SHINGO PUBLICATION AWARD

The Shingo Institute, part of the Jon M. Huntsman School of Business at Utah State University, is proud to announce that Dr. Morgan L. Jones has been awarded the Shingo Publication Award for his groundbreaking book, Believe. This award recognizes exceptional works that advance the understanding and application of the principles of organizational excellence.

Believe explores the transformative power of belief systems in shaping leadership behaviors and organizational outcomes, delivering a groundbreaking roadmap for transforming organizations from the inside out. Through compelling insights and practical frameworks, Dr. Jones challenges conventional thinking and inspires leaders to cultivate cultures rooted in purpose, trust, and continuous improvement. This inspiring book reveals how aligning personal values with organizational goals creates cultures that thrive rather than just survive. Through the innovative Mindset Framework, Jones shows how beliefs drive behaviors, and behaviors shape results, offering practical tools and real-world examples that make change achievable and sustainable. Complete with actionable strategies, Believe empowers leaders to unlock potential, foster trust, and ignite continuous improvement.

"Dr. Jones's work exemplifies the spirit of the Shingo Guiding Principles," said Ken Snyder, Executive Director of the Shingo Institute. "Believe provides a profound perspective on how beliefs drive behaviors, making it an invaluable resource for leaders committed to sustainable excellence."

Across the industry, thought leaders are calling Believe a must-read for anyone serious about driving sustainable organizational change:

Dr Jones hit the nail on the head again. *Believe* deals with the human element of a lean transformation journey in a case-rich environment and invites experimentation with practical frameworks. The book also gives practical advice for leaders coaching their teams towards excellence. This book will probably spend more time in the backpacks than the shelves.

Mauro Neves, CEO
Incitec Pivot Ltd
Shingo Institute Advisory Board Member

Morgan's book *Believe* offers practical insights and real-life examples useful for any leader who wants to use Lean tools and habits to improve customer experience and business performance. Most importantly, throughout his book, Morgan highlights that success is achieved by passionate people believing that change can happen, and it is worthwhile.

Carolyn McCann, Group Executive
Customer and Corporate Services – Westpac Group

The new book *Believe* fills a major void in the continuous improvement conversation. We often focus heavily on tools and avoid the difficult discussion about beliefs that influence behaviors and ultimately determine our results. This book can help advance the conversation on our continuous improvement journey.

Skip Steward, VP
Chief Improvement Officer
Baptist Memorial Healthcare Corporation

Morgan Jones has written a thoughtful book on how leaders' mindsets can either encourage or discourage effective improvement practices. He notes the importance of having a clear purpose. But more important than the words leaders express are the behaviors they practice on a day-in, day-out basis. Leaders' behaviors communicate what is really important.

Michael Bremer, VP AME Excellence Awards
Award Winning Author *How to Do a Gemba Walk*
and *Learn to See the Invisible*

This book is a valuable resource for anyone looking to improve organisational excellence. Crucially the book discusses the importance of mindset and behavior and provides practical tools and insights for leaders. Highly recommended.

Mike Allen, COO
National Bank of Australia

Morgan Jones has done it again. Another excellent book on how to better manage enterprises, taking his original thinking to a new level. A number of easily implementable ideas on becoming a better manager and leader.

Patrick Medley, Professor
University of Sydney
Managing Partner, Kedleton & Co

I found myself drifting off as I read Morgan's latest book. Not because it is boring, quite the opposite - as I read about belief and behavior, I reflected on situations and challenges in my own workplace and thought about how I can apply the ideas in the book. *Believe* is a valuable addition to the knowledge and skills of both experienced continuous improvement practitioners, those starting the journey and any leader wanting to transform organisational culture.

Dr Murray Wu, Director Strategy Systems
New Zealand Defence Force

Believe by Morgan Jones serves as a practical resource for leaders aiming to achieve sustainable organisational transformation. The book introduces a Mindset Framework that connects individual mindsets and behaviours to organisational processes and outcomes. Using real-world examples, case studies, and coaching techniques,

Jones illustrates how to translate the theory into practical strategies. This guide equips leaders with actionable insights for fostering continuous improvement and driving lasting transformative results in their organisations.

Rebecca Michalik, National President
Association of Manufacturing Excellence, Australia

Morgan brings together decades of learning and experience, to provide readers with a pragmatic and practical way to approach effective change management and driving high performance. Highly recommend!

Angelo Azar, COO
Honey Insurance

Such an inspiring book, the topic relating to the Shingo model was a great example of how things can be enhanced. Thought provoking the whole way through, real stories overlayed with conceptual thinking to enhance change and support people. We are all in service of our people, such a great read.

Rexine Jones, CFO
Hansen Yunchen

Dr. Morgan Jones's book *Believe* describes the connection between desired outcomes and mindsets using mental models, storytelling, and proof points. When you read *Believe*, you'll see how Dr. Jones draws connections between factors that are key in embedding change:

   a. the power of belief *and* creating good habits,
   b. the ability to perform good habits automatically *and* improved productivity,
   c. the 'outward circle' of behaviours to achieve enterprise excellence *and* the 'inward circle' of mindsets that drive our behaviours and habits.

Michelle Lue Reid
Chief Transformation Officer
IPH Ltd

Morgan Jones shares with us from a very personal perspective why ensuring individuals *Believe* is central to any organisation's progress and improvement. Having strongly made the case, Morgan then builds on the classic models of Enterprise Excellence and Organisational Heath to give us the framework for making this happen. At the centre of this is the principle of leaders being coaches, leading with humility and respecting the contribution of every individual. A true blend of culture and structure.

Jon Lindsay, Chair
The Executive Connection (TEC)
Director, Joined Up

In this fantastic book, Dr Jones teaches us how to build a culture aligned towards a common purpose through real world examples. Processes and infrastructure must be aligned with company goals and supported by a common enterprise-wide model for excellence. The mindset framework, coaching framework and operating system case studies help us move from the "why" to the "how" of operational excellence.

Tolan Brown
VP, Supply Chain
O.C. Tanner Company

Morgan has written a book about lean leadership that takes us on a journey around the world of lean transformation by explaining the key concepts of lean leadership interwoven with real world examples and lessons from experts. The book can serve as an introduction for those interested in leading change and a reference guide to ground even the experienced sensei in the roots of lean. The real-world examples and illustrations help understand the why behind successful transformations and path to success.

Arne Vogt, COO
Vitesse Systems

Believe is a considered and insightful practical illustration of how behaviour, influenced by a healthy mindset and reinforced by intrinsic motivation, developed through habitual practice, drives sustainable and tangible outcomes. Dr Jones has created a thought-provoking text that is brought to life with relevant case studies and self-learning exercises. An excellent addition to a business leaders toolkit.

Ellie Atkinson
Managing Director, Performance Improvement

Morgan has done it again with another inciteful and highly practical guide to successfully embedding Continuous Improvement in an organisation. Building on 4+1 approach from his previous work, he unlocks the key to sustainable cultural change is not just about tools and metrics, but engaging employee's spirit, morale and importantly BELIEF as a motivator for change. This is essential reading for anyone undertaking transformational work to learn from many great examples and experiences that Morgan has.

Martin Fletcher, GM
Customer Process Transformation, Bupa

Embedding improvement in a business is more crucial now than ever, but some efforts are more successful than others. Morgan leverages his extensive experience to offer practical insights and real-world examples, illustrating the significant impact that the right habits can have on achieving better outcomes. This book is a must-read for any leader committed to enhancing their business and understanding the habits necessary for sustainable improvement.

Christian Dalle Nogare
Managing Director, CI Sustain

Underneath lean systems and processes are mindsets and behaviours and underneath them are beliefs. Beliefs are the inexhaustible fuel that when connected with everything above drives improvement at a peerless level. *Believe* deeply describes this relationship and what it takes to connect the fuel source to the engine

Rob Telford, VP
Group Operations, BHP

Believe

believe

The one simple area of focus that can make
your transformations and Continuous
Improvement culture truly sustainable

DR MORGAN L. JONES

Cover design by BookPOD and Action New Thinking

ISBN: 978-0-9873477-7-0 (hbk) ISBN: 978-0-9873477-8-7 (pbk)
ISBN: 978-0-9873477-9-4 (ebook)

 A catalogue record for this book is available from the National Library of Australia

Book proceeds will be donated to Dementia Australia.

Dementia Australia is the national peak body supporting people living with dementia, their families, and carers. More than 421,000 Australians live with dementia, and more than 1.6 million people participate in their care. Dementia is the second leading cause of death in Australia and will likely soon become the first, yet it remains a challenging and often misunderstood condition.

Dementia Australia responds to this challenge with trusted information, education, and support services. They support vital research and health workers providing essential care and equip communities with tools and knowledge to make our society more dementia friendly. We are here to support people impacted by dementia and to enable them to live as well as possible.

www.dementia.org.au

"Fundamentally, we don't just need to know *what* to do and how to do it; we need to know why we are doing it and then believe in that why and the how."

Dr Morgan Jones, 35th Shingo Conference, Provo 2023.

Acknowledgments

I would like to thank so many people who have helped me develop my thinking over the years. There are too many to name. Specifically, in compiling this book, I would like to thank Mike Allen, Ellie Atkinson, Angelo Azar, Michael Bremer, Tolan Brown, Bob Carter, Tina Chawner, Warren Cotter, Steve Dargan, Martin Fletcher, Carmen Irwin, Brad Jeavons, Rexine Jones, Jon Lindsay, Carolyn McCann, Mick McKay, Prof Patrick Medley, Rebecca Michalik, Mauro Neves, Christian Dalle Nogare, Evan Powell, Michelle Lue Reid, Ken Snyder, Skip Steward, Rob Telford, Xiang Teo, Arne Vogt, and Dr Murray Wu.

Contents

Foreword

Shigeo Shingo (1909-1990) was a Japanese industrial engineer whose influence extends globally in the field of organizational and operational excellence. He is renowned for inventing terms such as SMED (single-minute exchange of dies), *poka-yoke* (a Japanese idiom meaning "error-proofing"), and one-piece flow production — which Shingo referred to as "non-stock production." He authored 18 books and in 1988, Utah State University in the United States presented Shingo with an honorary doctorate. The university established the Shingo Prize in his name to recognize outstanding organizations for their operational and organizational excellence. I am privileged to serve as the Executive Director of the Shingo Institute, the organization that oversees the Shingo Prize.

While Shingo was famous for things like SMED and the poka-yoke, he taught many other profound concepts, including that there is always a better way. Shingo studied Henry Ford's practices and Ford's thinking can be identified in much of what Shingo taught about there being a better way. As Ford famously said, "Whether you think you can or you think you can't – you're right."

This mindset leads directly to the purpose of this book – i.e. to believe. Ford's saying could easily be restated in terms of belief:

> "Whether you believe you can or you believe you can't – you're right."

Shingo argues that we cannot ever stop believing in there being a better way. He was annoyed when people told him that they identified the "best way" or "we've always done it that way, and it works fine" and explains some key barricades to people who do not believe there is a better way.

First, Shingo teaches us that we need to believe that a better way is possible:

> "If we want to achieve improvement, we must first have the mental flexibility to believe that even though there is only one summit, there are many paths we can tread to reach it. If we adamantly think that the current methods are the best and no other means are possible, improvement ideas will never emerge." [1]

Second, people believe that because they have already identified a better way, they believe that an even *better* way is not possible. Shingo teaches us that we have to believe there is always a possible better way:

> "People sometimes mistakenly believe intermediate-level improvements are ultimate improvements. If they have raised to 80 percent, what used to be 50 percent, they tend to think of that as a limit. They overlook the fact that it can be increased to 100 percent." [2]

Third, people believe that there is only one way — and they believe that until they find that one perfect way, they should not make any changes. Shingo teaches us that we need to believe that there are always many possible improvement methods:

> "Progress will never pay a visit to those who stubbornly insist that their way is right and no other means are possible. Yet if we keep an open mind and believe that there are several possible means to each end,

---

1 Shingo, Shigeo, *Kaizen and the Art of Creative* Thinking, 2007, Enna Products Corporation and PCS Inc., p. 85-86.

2 Shingo, Shigeo, *The Shingo Production Management System*, 1992, Productivity Press Inc., translated by Andrew P. Dillon, p. xxii.

improvement ideas will emerge through the process of selecting the best method."[3]

Shingo further explains:

> "No improvement could take place in this world if there were only a single means to each end. Indeed, it is only when one believes in the existence of multiple means that the possibility of improvement first appears."[4]

Shingo clearly and unequivocally endorses the scientific method through such teachings. So much of our efforts to improve our organizations are based on our beliefs – whether we believe we can or we believe we can't. Shingo argues for *believing you can.*

In this book, Dr. Morgan Jones explores the various facets of belief as it pertains to organizational excellence. It will help strengthen your resolve to believe you can.

Ken Snyder
Executive Director
Shingo Institute
Jon M. Huntsman School of Business
Utah State University
Logan, Utah, USA

---

3   Shingo, Shigeo, *Non-Stock Production: The Shingo System for Continuous Improvement*, 1988, Productivity Press, translated by Andrew P. Dillon, p. 109; emphasis added.

4   Robinson, Alan, *The Shingo System: Modern Approaches to Manufacturing Improvement*, 1990, Productivity, Inc., p. 123; emphasis added.

Inspiration for Writing This Book

The situation that inspired my thinking around this book goes back about 15 years, when I was asked to fix safety at our Pacific Island industrial facility. Local workers refused to wear Personal Protective Equipment (PPE) even though it was mandated to be worn. After spending time with the workers both in the work environment and their villages and in discussion with the village elders, we agreed that the workers needed to believe in the use of PPE.

After lots of consultation, the solution came down to adding a simple pocket (Plenert) onto the workers' high-viz shirts with a picture of their family. The underlying belief of why workers came to work was to support their families. If they become injured, they might not be able to continue to provide in the future. The pictures provided a visual representation of family, beliefs, and values. Remarkably, this transformed the use of PPE within one week and reduced injuries by 78% and lost time injuries to zero. I smiled at the cultural element as workers stopped straight outside the gate, removed their steel toe-capped boots, and walked home barefoot. Once they understood the what, how, and why and then believed in the way, they took accountability to make sure everyone went home every day without injuring their family and impacting their broader village community.

There is also a personal reason behind the core of *Believe* that goes back to my childhood. I was born in Zambia, and my father worked in mining with large crews of local people working for him. One day, there was an incident and my father saved the life of one of these workers, who just so happened to be the chief of a local Zulu prince. My father was honored by the tribe, and we had many interactions with them. They taught me a greeting they had:

"Sawa Bona."

This literally translates to "I see you." However, the intent of this greeting was far deeper:

"I see where you have come from, your past, I see who you are today before me, your present, and I see your future, your potential."

This has had a profound impact on how I see and interact with people, not only seeing who they are but 'believing' in their potential.

Introduction to Why Beliefs Are Important

I have visited many organizations over the years, most recently those that are challenging for the Shingo Prize or have received an excellence award. There is one thing that stands out for me, and it is how mature organizations feel when you walk into their workplace. It is hard to explain, but it was definitely a felt experience. While there, I explored the behaviors, corporate/charter values and principles. The distinguishing factor in very mature organizations, for example, Abbott Industries, Jabil, BHP, etc., is that there is a mutual understanding of the beliefs that underpin their principles and values. It's not overly documented, just consistent. In less mature organizations, values and principles might be clearly stated, but employees often repeat them without grasping the underlying reasons or beliefs. This lack of understanding prevents these ideal behaviors from becoming 'habits'.

Why is change so difficult? Organizations spend incredible amounts of time and money working on change, trying to become better: more efficient, more sustainable, more customer- and environmentally friendly. Why do up to 80% of lean transformations fail? (Plenert G. 2021 and Plenert J 2023). Why is change so challenging in so many cases? I suggest they miss what people must believe to make the transformation or change successful.

As we will see in this book, by far, the most important big-picture mistake organizations make when they tackle change is focusing on *tools* and *compliance.* No doubt you've been through many of these change management initiatives: the meetings, the company briefs and emails, the change metrics and performance benchmarks... all of these are yardsticks designed to measure what you and everyone else at your company did during the change process, and whether you followed the prescribed method or not.

Measurements and yardsticks have their place, but there's something fundamental missing from the standard method most organizations adopt when trying to manage change, and that is spirit. The problem with the method-focused approach to human behavior is that it fails to inspire and create belief for change. There is often a 'can't-see-the-forest-for-the-trees' problem since most organizations focus on the methodology rather than the underlying thought processes and behaviors that result from them.

If you tell your employees to follow the steps in the manual and submit progress reports, they'll no doubt do their best to follow and comply—but therein lies the problem. By focusing on compliance, you're neglecting to connect with them at a deeper level: motivation, the motivation that can drive lasting behavioral, habitual change.

With this in mind, let's try to understand how and why so many lean transformations fail—and how we can motivate people to make the changes necessary to ensure success. While various sources give different figures, what is abundantly clear and has been for many years is that organizations usually do not achieve satisfactory, lasting change or realize transformation. One theme that emerges is that it is difficult for most organizations to achieve a sustained sense of momentum after the initial implementation of whatever project they have chosen to undertake.

Figure 0.1 shows the usual improvement curve of organizations that rises and then starts to decline. Years ago, the Shingo Institute noticed a common trend among organizations that were driving a culture of continuous improvement, and initial gains were often accompanied by a swift decline (Plenert 2017).

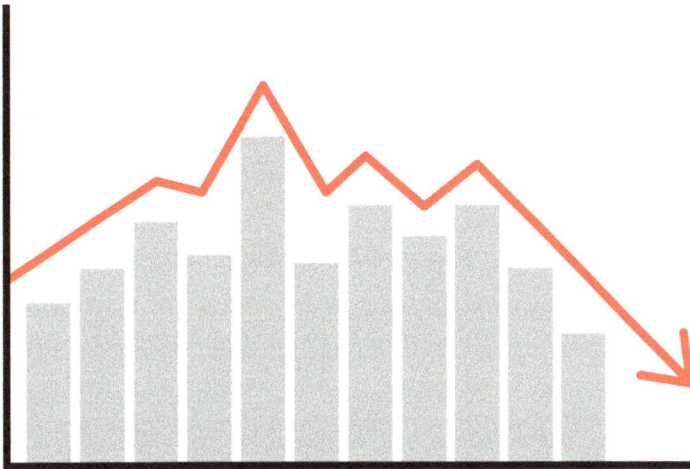

Figure 0.1—Typical performance improvement curve (Plenert 2017)

There are several key reasons so many lean transformations fail.

- Implementation of a tool-oriented approach, one that focuses on tools rather than culture.
- Focus on performance at the expense of looking at the health of the organization.
- No continuous tracking and measuring of health impacts.
- In a related vein, lack of motivation is another key reason lean transformations fail.

- Poor communication: inconsistent or ineffective communication fails to convince people of the fundamental need for changed behavior.

Researchers who study lean transformations have long been aware of these issues, and many have suggested a variety of so-called Critical Success Factors (CSFs). A CSF is that it is one of a handful of things that must go well if an organization or a manager is to succeed. While lists of CSFs may vary, there is broad consensus among researchers about how to correctly define a CSF and even a consensus about some of the most important CSFs (Netland, 2015).

What have researchers discovered regarding CSFs for organizational improvement initiatives? The answer, according to Netland (2015), is that the three most important CSFs are: "management commitment and involvement," "training and education," and "employee participation and empowerment." These critical success factors (CSFs) all share a profound common focus on intrinsic motivation and morale.

Another aspect of this is contingency, i.e., how much an environment's particulars affect the implementation of CSFs. Contingency theory is somewhat in tension with CSFs since it contends that different environments are likely to require different approaches (Netland, 2015). However, this does not mean CSFs are not relevant: it suggests that they will be most effective if they are tailored to the environment.

Contingency theory can hone the use of CSFs by clarifying the details that define them. Different corporations operating in different industries and serving different markets are likely to see different CSFs as important for implementing lean initiatives. Despite variations in implementation, there remains a consensus on the primary critical success factors (CSFs).

However, adapting to an organization's specific context is essential, as highlighted by Netland (2015).

Another important takeaway from this research is that change management is more likely to succeed if management takes seriously active leadership and support. People need guidance, and one of the most important parts of management is providing guidance (Jones et al., 2023). While some of this guidance can and should be teaching employees about processes and metrics, what employees need to see is that management is invested in helping to create and promote change by modeling it. If leaders are not defining, role modeling, and reinforcing the desired behaviors they want to see because of the change management, then how are employees to understand that these are the desired behaviors and something in which they should believe?

One thing to understand here is that actions do matter more than words. In many ways, employees will care about words to the degree that they match up with actions. Organizations that want to drive change must be led by people committed to modeling that change and inspiring people to carry it out. The behaviors a leader shows, the actions they take, the things they choose to support or to ignore—all these things matter immensely when implementing change.

Crucially, what this means is that a leader cannot afford to be passive about creating and managing organizational culture. A leader cannot, for example, treat organizational culture as another thing to manage. A leader should not give control of organizational culture to another department, for example, HR. Instead, leaders must lead culture: they must be culture-definers, influencers, and transformers. This is the catalyst between successful and unsuccessful culture transformations. I love this quote that illustrates this point: "The only thing of real importance that *leaders do is to create and manage culture." If you do not manage culture, it manages you,* and you may not even be aware of the extent to which this is happening." A quote from Edgar Schein, *Professor, MIT Sloan School of Management and quoted in the Discover Excellence book (Plenert, 2017).*

Given the importance of organizational culture, why is it so challenging for so many leaders to transform it? Part of the answer is the inherent complexity of organizational culture; it takes substantial commitment and effort to change a culture, and leaders must commit to long-term behavior modification to model a cultural transformation sufficient for it to stick. There is also general human reluctance to change under most circumstances: if people are used to a way of doing things, it takes time and effort to persuade them and change their belief in the necessity for change. The greater, more effortful, and more complex the change, the harder it will generally be to convince people to commit to the change and redefine the organization.

Knowing the innate human preference for the familiar and the reluctance to change, we can better understand the main dynamics at work in the high rates of failure of transformations. This is because organizations usually have an innate maintenance of the status quo regarding established culture; people perceive change as incurring costs—the extra effort required to figure out the change and perform it—and every change comes with risk. Changes sometimes impose steep costs for little or very questionable benefits.

By understanding this innate source of reluctance to change, leaders can work with employees, rather than against them, in modeling change. Leaders who model the behavioral framework they want to see in the new, changed environment will succeed far more in making their change initiatives. This requires leaders to have the skills, the capability, and the systems in place to enact the change and carry it out over the long term.

Organizational change inherently involves risk, and mitigating those risks is crucial to safeguard a company's competitive position. However, leaders must also embrace calculated risks, recognizing that without risk, there can be no substantial reward. The key lies in fostering a risk-aware mindset—one that enables leaders to navigate risks effectively while minimizing potential harm. Transparency about risk is equally vital in change management; informed and empowered employees can contribute to risk awareness and effective risk navigation.

Beyond managing risks, change management must be proactive and planned out in advance. The organization must have a clear idea about what is changing, why, and what the roles of all parties will be before the change management initiative is rolled out. Change management also should be within the organization: a successful change management initiative ultimately depends on everyone seeing the change as simply how the organization works. This will take effort, which is again why leadership modeling the changes and showing them in action is so important.

This highlights the importance of ensuring the change readiness of the organization, site, or department before starting the change. Create the awareness and desire to believe in the change.

Again, as can be seen, organizations and people usually possess an innate conservatism about change. They see it as an additional effort, and they are predisposed to not seeing it as necessary. Then, the role of leadership is to challenge employees and encourage them to find good reasons to question and push back against the status quo in an organization. This takes us back to the role of leadership in inspiring: inspired and empowered employees will be more likely to consider the possibility that things could be done in a better fashion, and this invites consideration of a positive vision for a better future.

That means the outcome of the lean transformation must be one of teaching people to see that they have a second job while at work: improving the job they are hired to do, making it better tomorrow than today. Leaders who model this in their behavior and reward it in the workplace will go far when implementing lean transformations. Crucially, this means that organizations must shift the focus of incentives: the emphasis must be on skill appraisal, development, and rectification of deficiencies, though there must also be a focus on intrinsic motivations.

Changing organizational culture ultimately requires a focus on the interaction between motivation and behaviors. A key thing to understand here is that motivation affects mindsets, and mindsets are important for driving consistent beliefs and behaviors. Teach people to have the right mindset so that they will hold the desired beliefs and genuinely want to perform the desired behaviors.

To give an example of this idea discussed by Jones et al. (2023), a luminescent printer manufacturer hired one of the authors to help increase the quality of their output and resolve their failure rate of 13 percent, which led them to overbuild everything by 20 percent. The core problem was that the motivations of the employees were fear-based: none of the floor employees were comfortable with making changes on their own since everything had to be directed to supervisors. The function of the employees in this company was to produce parts, which meant that their knowledge and experience were not being respected or honored.

The solution was to shift the organization's culture in a way that demonstrated respect for the knowledge and experience of the employees. Management needed to show humility: after all, the employees better understood the functions of their roles than management did. This message was paired with a broader organizational vision consisting of a set of goals such that everyone could understand their part of the broader picture. After that, the employees could be trained on lean techniques, such as value stream mapping and so on. The result was a decrease in defect rate, from 13 percent to 2 percent, and a 20 percent increase in capacity. The company maintained the change and eventually reduced the failure rate to one-half percent (Jones et al., 2023).

The main lesson of this organizational change initiative is that it is possible to enact meaningful change when people feel respected and valued for their knowledge and skills. When management shows humility and a willingness to listen to employees, this creates a context in which employees are more likely to be receptive to a big-picture vision for change, one in which they will have to play a carefully specified and significant part. Employees who are incentivized in this manner will also be more receptive to learning about new techniques for lean change management and implementing those techniques on an ongoing basis.

This book opened this introduction by talking about the key mistakes that organizations make when they focus on tools and compliance rather than spirit and morale to create **belief**. The essential distinction lies in recognizing that tools and adherence to metrics do matter, but the primary focus should be on understanding the underlying motivations for change. Effective change involves engaging employees, respecting their knowledge and skills, and demonstrating humility.

Human behaviour tells us people follow those they respect, and that respect and humility play pivotal roles in effective leadership. When leaders model these qualities, they inspire respect from their employees. As a result, employees become willing partners in change rather than feeling coerced by authority. By fostering such an environment, leaders create the foundation for a successful, change-oriented organizational culture—one that can tackle large-scale, complex changes and sustain them over time.

We will see repeatedly throughout this book if you want to change the organizational culture, you need first to address the underlying mindset, the spirit, the morale, the belief, and the organizational readiness. Once you manage that, you'll be working with confident, motivated employees who want to help the change initiative succeed.

1

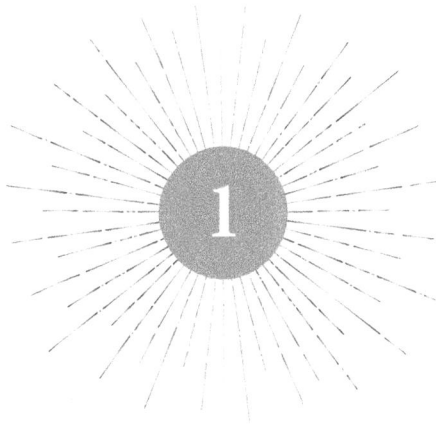

The Outward Circle

At the core of every successful change management or transformation initiative is an understanding of one simple principle: the health of an organization determines almost everything (Jones et al., 2023). Because change inevitably represents risk, it is imperative to understand how well-prepared the organization's employees, processes, and infrastructure are before starting a continuous improvement initiative. A healthy organization is one in which the motivations and capabilities of the organization's people—employees and management—are aligned and in which the processes and infrastructure can support the organization's goals.

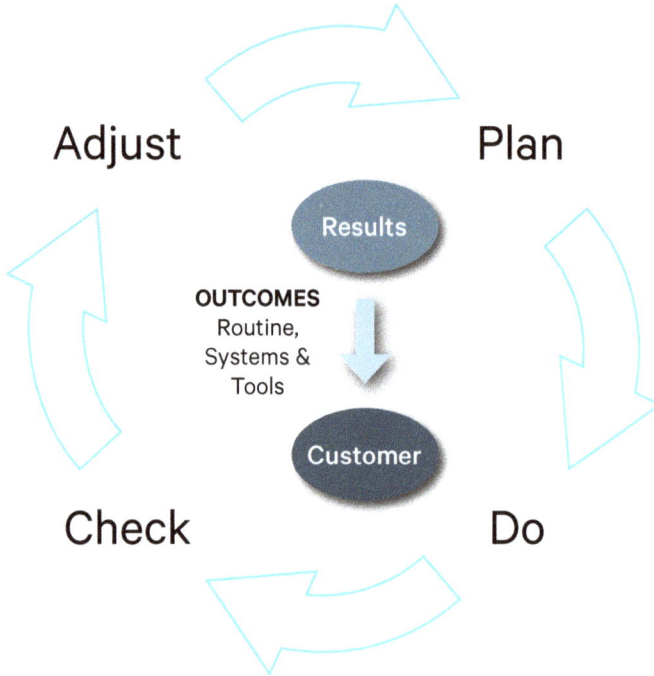

Figure 1.1—Driving results for customers (©Action New Thinking)

Figure 1.1 shows how some organizations get initial improvements by getting clarity on customer expectations of results. The failure of so many companies to understand this before starting a continuous improvement program concerns a fundamental inability to connect plans to the objective reality of the real world beyond the executive level. However, companies that engage with reality in proactive ways are better positioned to achieve ongoing continuous improvement that actually impacts and improves behaviors (Jones et al., 2023).

An important aspect of this is motivation, i.e., incentives. Consider the example given by Jones et al. (2023) of an organization planning to close one of its plants—and naturally, choosing the one with the worst quality record. The manager wanted one of the authors to tell them why their quality was so poor—after all, they had a quality department, quality training for all employees, and banners throughout the facility that reminded all employees of the importance of quality.

When the author asked the manager what the employees were measured on, the manager said they were measured on units produced: they received bonuses based on their output. The author spotted the obvious problem with this scheme: the plant incentivized employees to produce more units in less time, meaning they were optimizing for speed rather than quality. And why would the employees need to worry about quality since there was a quality department? (Jones et al., 2023).

The key lesson here is that if you want to understand behavior, you need to understand the incentive structure that behavior is designed to respond to. Organizations are not simply sub-optimal or dysfunctional for no reason: the people who make up those organizations have their reasons for doing exactly what they are doing. If employees are consistently being inefficient or ineffective, there is some reason or set of reasons they believe to be in their best interest. The same is true of management.

The result was a dysfunctional plant. Scheduling was a nightmare, with the American expeditors changing production schedules to try to push rush jobs through the plant, only for the advisors to make adjustments before top management did the same. Middle management positions were often filled through nepotism. Strikes were frequent, deliveries of raw materials were sporadic, and equipment repair included scavenging for spare parts.

Another excellent example comes from Plenert (2021), who describes a case involving a factory in Mexico. The 6,000-employee factory had numerous problems installing a production control system like those used in the United States. Factors contributing to the difficulty included an unskilled workforce, poor power supplies, and difficulties with employee-management relations. One key problem was the intense stratification on the basis of nationality, language, culture, and education: the firm's top management were all United States citizens, as were a number of expeditors and advisors they sent in, while the secondary levels were primarily Mexican citizens, albeit trained or educated in the United States. The workers were Mexican nationals, and the vast majority were unskilled, so they had trouble filling out time sheets.

Not surprisingly, relations between the three groups were characterized by tensions, resentment, and contempt. The unskilled Mexican laborers resent their affluent, US-educated Mexican bosses, who looked down on them in turn. The workers also resented the American upper management, who had to use interpreters to communicate and who made them feel inadequate. Given these resentments and antipathies, it is perhaps a small wonder that the workers and the company had profoundly different motivations and goals—specifically, workers did not see themselves as part of the company and wanted to spend as much time with family as possible. This often meant that after receiving paychecks, the workers would avoid work for several days, returning only when they felt a financial necessity.

What can one do about an organizational environment that is so profoundly dysfunctional? For Plenert, the answer was to address the levels of dysfunctional behavior in ways that aligned people, processes, and production. Because the workforce was unskilled, the author recommended simplified input documents and tools that did not require written information. For middle management, the author recommended training on manufacturing production and control topics, including which metrics were critical. To improve relations between labor and management, the author recommended open sharing of information and helping employees to understand what the information was telling them. However, all of that changed when company management began to turn the problem around and saw manure not as waste but rather as a commodity. Executive chairperson Charlie Mort was certainly aware that manure could be used for fertilizer. Still, the problem was that there were regulatory issues with this. Between that and issues with dry times, the manure could really only serve markets within about 40 kilometers around the feedlot. However, Mort & Co. did not want that to be the end of it, so they have been working on a new solution: turning the manure into organic granules (Baczkowski, 2023).

Other recommendations the author provided targeted issues with machinery, unreliable power supplies, etc.

After the initial rush of benefits of the basic application of tools and routine discipline in Figure 1.1, organizations start to migrate to defining and embedding the ideal or core behaviors they want and need to embed sustainable results.

The core lesson to internalize here is the entire idea of the outward wheel: instead of merely looking at the company's plans and the schemas and ideas in the minds of senior managers, expeditors, advisors, middle managers, and employees, the author analyzed behavior in terms of incentives. By observing what was going on in the real world as well as understanding the mentalities of the groups, the author gained a better understanding of what was wrong and how to improve upon it. This is exactly the reality-based thinking that is imperative if an organization is to implement and maintain a continuous improvement project. Culture can be interpreted through four subdomains: Guiding Principles, Systems, Tools, and Results (Plenert, 2021). Figure 1.2 shows the Shingo model from Discover Excellence (Plenert 2017).

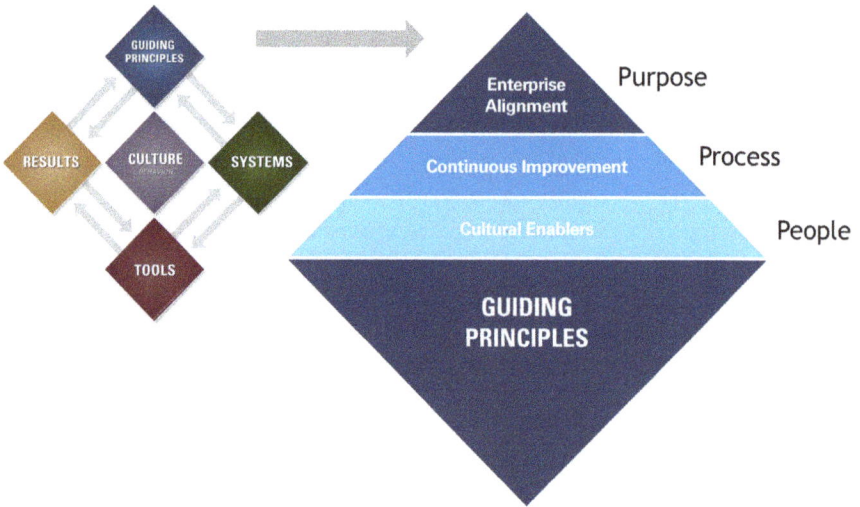

Figure 1.2—Shingo Model (Plenert (2017)

Now that we're in the realm of reality-based thinking geared towards the creation of better results, it's time to remember the overarching purpose of being in business: to serve customers. We can apply this outward wheel thinking to align results with customers and to see the customer as our front line. Once we have this shift in mindset, we can use simple Lean/Agile tools to improve results.

We can think of this in terms of optimizing for better outcomes regarding routines, systems, and tools and using that optimization to align results with customers better (see Figure 1.1). Given the right discipline and the right optimization, we can accomplish improved outcomes that are better aligned with consumers. And what do consumers want? Good news: If you ask them, they'll tell you!

The beautiful thing here is that conceptually, this is all simple: behavior is what we do and say that others can observe, so if we behave in the right manner, we can get a result, and we can take that result to the customer. If the customer likes the result, they'll tell us. Then we can do more of that behavior—and along the way, we can optimize the routine, systems, and tools we need to produce more of that behavior and do it even better. Over time, this becomes a cycle—namely, the outward circle we've been discussing.

A great example of this comes from the owners of Queensland, Australia-based feedlot Mort & Co. Being the largest feedlot in Australia, they used to have one of the largest manure removal issues— after all, the feedlot regularly accommodated nearly 80,000 cattle at any one time. The combined efforts of nearly 80,000 cattle are sufficient to produce 100,000 tons of manure in the course of a year, and until very recently, this was a problem for the company: it was, after all, waste (Baczkowski, 2023).

But all of that changed when company management began to turn the problem around and see manure not as waste but rather as a commodity. Executive chairperson Charlie Mort was certainly aware that manure could be used for fertilizer. Still, the problem was that there were regulatory issues with this. Between that and issues with dry times, the manure could really only serve markets about 40 kilometers around the feedlot. However, Mort & Co did not want that to be the end of it, so they have been working on a new solution: turning the manure into organic granules (Baczkowski, 2023).

The genius of this is that most Australian soils are naturally low in the organic forms of carbon that plants need to grow—but the granules, which are suitable for organic fertilizer, are 30% organic carbon. This means they're an excellent way to repurpose a waste product—one that could create environmental issues—into an asset that farmers actually want to buy. Their initial pilot plant turned out 10-kilogram batches, and now their factory produces five tons an hour. An additional benefit is that for various reasons—climate, soil fertility, established patterns of use—the production of animal manures is usually concentrated in the same general areas with the greatest requirements for fertilizers for farming, which reduces costs and emissions about long-haul transport of fertilizers (Baczkowski, 2023).

Mort & Co.'s example is a good example of how to align results with customers: create value for your customers and optimize along those lines. One model that provides a helpful methodology for this optimization is the Shingo Model, named after Dr. Shigeo Shingo (Plenert, 2021). The model centers on the culture of an organization, which is defined by behavior—culture is as culture does.

The interactions between the four subdomains are also worth understanding: Guiding Principles align with Systems, which drive Guiding Principles. Systems select Tools, and Tools enable Systems. Tools are necessary to achieve results, and results help refine tools. Finally, Results affirm Guiding Principles, which also drive Results. One way to simplify the insights of this profound model is to observe that ideal results, measured by Key Performance Indicators (KPIs), require ideal behavior or Key Behavioral Indicators (KBIs). The Shingo Institute has the first of three insights into organizational excellence, and the second is that purpose and systems drive behavior. Finally, the third is that principles inform ideal behavior. Figure 1.3 shows this graphically.

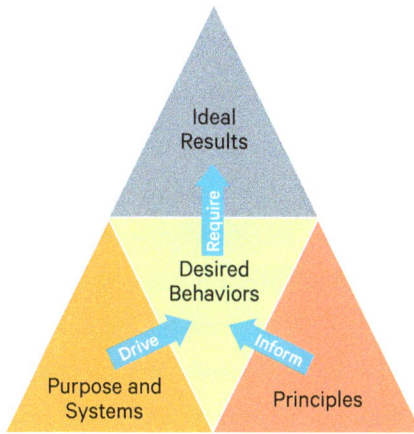

Figure 1.3—Shingo 3 Insights (Jones et al., 2022)

The Shingo Institute has been trying to help organizations achieve Enterprise Excellence for decades. However, as we have discussed, the Institute has noted that most such initiatives fail. To help those organizations that are serious about Enterprise Excellence, the Institute has created a roadmap, starting with defining what Enterprise Excellence means for an organization.

For a good introduction to the Shingo Institute's methodology, consider this anecdote about a Japanese Toyota executive who was asked why his firm was so willing to share its secrets. He answered that by the time other companies figured out how to do what Toyota was doing, they would have innovated to the point that the other companies would still be decades behind. This anecdote illuminates an essential aspect of the Shingo philosophy of continuous improvement: either a company is trying to innovate and improve constantly, or it believes it is too busy to "waste" time on making changes. The first type sees stagnancy and tradition as gateways to becoming moribund and failing, while the second is doomed to bankruptcy.

Business history is littered with examples of businesses that did not anticipate major innovations and were crushed by them. Think of Blockbuster, the one-time king of video rentals that passed on the chance to buy Netflix and was later crushed by it. Blockbuster did not anticipate the consequences of mail-ordering DVD subscription services with no late fees and the rise of streaming. Similarly, NCR felt secure as a manufacturer of mechanical calculators—until IBM came along. IBM itself mistakenly thought that smaller personal computers were not commercially feasible and was devoured by Apple and Microsoft. The lesson is stark: either your company will pursue continuous improvement and innovation, or another company will crush it.

What makes the Shingo Institute's model so unique as a method for helping organizations embrace continuous change is the emphasis on integrating cultural change with systems changes, metrics changes, and overall consistency such that the changes are sustainable. And crucially, at the center of the model is the element of culture. This is because the other elements depend on culture: if the culture of an organization is not one of continuous improvement, innovation, and excellence, then the people who make up that organization will do what humans have always done and revert to familiar, tried-and-true patterns.

The reason for this is simple: humans like familiarity. Left to our own devices, we revert to familiar patterns because they are comfortable, known quantities. Thus, the first thing an organization must do if it wants to embrace continuous improvement is to create a transformed culture. This is sooner said than done: a company must articulate a clear vision of what that desired culture looks like and then structure goals aimed at accomplishing that culture. It must also have systems that support the movement toward and maintenance of this culture, and there must be metrics that motivate people to work toward the desired culture and encourage behaviors that help achieve and sustain it.

Culture transformation is not a one-and-done process. It is a campaign marked by intense, ongoing effort exerted over the years. Crucially, it also occurs in stages. It is common for even the most successful companies to have long track records of things they have tried and often failed at. Those companies are companies that continue to work toward excellence no matter what, trying various things, keeping what works, and discarding what does not work until they arrive at something that performs well. Once they have a thing that works well, they tweak it and try to improve it—and they continue to repeat this process, becoming increasingly excellent as they improve their ability to improve continuously.

Where to begin this process? The Shingo Institute's answer is to start by defining Guiding Principles (capitalization intentional) that will be universal and timeless, applying to everything an organization is doing and serving to define the identity of the organization (Figure 4.2). These principles include cultural enablers, processes for continuous improvement, and the whole alignment of the enterprise, which must be focused on creating value for the customer. The purpose of the method is to orient the organization toward the Guiding Principles so the organization can use them to orient itself toward excellence (Plenert, 2021).

Once an organization is oriented toward these guiding principles, the enterprise goals should look very different than they would be without them. The goals will no longer be conceptualized in terms of financial benchmarks and milestones. Instead, they will be concerned with employees, customers, safety, and quality, and all in very specific, actionable, measurable ways. Rather than "Safety First" or "Satisfied

Customers," the organization will be oriented toward specific safety- and customer- goals that foster continuous improvement. What does it mean to be safe? How do we know if we have satisfied the customer? This change in mindset will serve as the foundation for facilitating a great deal more change.

These ideas are further developed and elaborated in the three key transformation insights that define the Guiding Principles (Shingo Institute, Plenert 2017). The first insight is that ideal results require ideal behaviors. The key thing here is that achievements are themselves the consequences of behavior. An organization that has developed guiding principles sufficient to create a positive growth culture can adjust employee behavior in ways that will actually deliver the ideal results, which is the result the organization needs to become continuously innovative and competitive. The expectations must condition everyone to seek and practice ideal behavior: the ideal must become the norm.

The second insight is that purpose and systems drive behavior. There's an elegant simplicity to this one: the beliefs people have define purpose, and purpose defines systems with such a profound effect on how employees behave in the workplace. Every day, an employee goes to work and interacts with various systems that help them figure out what to believe about the organization, their place in it, the work that they do, and what to believe about management. One part of this that is worth understanding is that in many cases—perhaps virtually all—employees can, with enough cooperation and ingenuity, make any metric look good if they believe management thinks that metric is important. This is all the truer if they believe their performance will be evaluated based on that number.

Too often, system designs do not consider the behavioral consequences of the systems. This creates opportunities for employees to make metrics look good, whether or not they are actually good, and whether or not they measure anything important—or the right thing. For management, the task is to realign management, improvement, and work systems so that the ideal behaviors result. Employees will then be oriented toward those behaviors and not toward massaging metrics.

The third great insight is that principles inform ideal behavior. A principle is a foundational rule with a consequence, and the more employees understand and internalize it, the better they will behave. Management must show the importance of these principles in their behavior and provide employees with education and support to grow in their ability to live by them as well. Together, these three insights can propel an organization toward continuous improvement and innovation—if the organization commits to implementing them and building on them.

Change

It's not that people have an absolute distaste for change. We like change, especially when it's for the better. We don't like the fear of what potential change will bring to us.

This quote from George Shinn sums it up:

> "Growth means change, and change involves risk stepping from the known to the unknown."

This is why change in the workplace is often met with resistance and apprehension. Human nature resists the unfamiliar, and change uncertainty can be unsettling.

Understanding why change is difficult for people and adopting effective change practices to help with it can ease any transition. This will make the process more manageable. Here's what we don't like:

1. Change disrupts our established routines and habits, creating a sense of instability.
2. People grow accustomed to a particular way of working, and ANY deviation from it can be met with resistance.
3. The fear of the unknown causes uncertainty about roles, job security, or the need to learn new skills.

Leaders must get ahead of all change efforts and focus on clear communication to navigate these challenges. Being transparent with the reasons for the change, detailing its anticipated benefits, and promoting the roadmap for implementation can alleviate uncertainty.

Providing regular updates before, during, and after any change effort can ease tensions. Open forums and town hall meetings allow team members to express their concerns and be heard. Another factor contributing to this resistance is the difficulty of leaving one's comfort zone. Change often requires us to step outside the familiar, which can be anxiety-inducing. Leaders can help us by providing training and resources to support us in acquiring new skills.

Assigning people mentors and creating a culture of continuous learning can also minimize the impact of change. Change should be considered an opportunity for personal and professional growth. Involving team members in the change process from the outset can also enhance acceptance. Soliciting input, encouraging feedback, and integrating team member perspectives into planning makes individuals feel valued. It gets them invested in the change.

Summary

Recognizing and celebrating accomplishments during the change is another effective practice. Acknowledging the efforts of the people affected helps build morale and reinforces transformative growth's positive aspects.

Change in the workplace is a multifaceted challenge that demands thoughtful leadership. Understanding the barriers and adopting practices such as the ones shared here can support leaders in helping with successful transitions.

As we have seen in this chapter, every continuous improvement project is an exercise in embracing change and the inevitable risk that change brings. Healthy organizations understand this reality and adapt to it, aligning people's motivations and capabilities toward the organization's goals. Improvement must have a direction, and in this case, this means a clear understanding of customer expectations followed by the creation of incentives to ensure everyone is working in the correct direction in a way that is actually conducive to improvement on an ongoing basis. In our discussion incentives, misaligned incentives are fundamental to, if not the entire reason for, patterns of dysfunctional and suboptimal behavior. Organizations that understand this are better equipped to create incentives that align with the behaviors that the organization needs to encourage if it is actually to improve. As we have seen, purpose and systems drive behavior. This is the logic of the outward circle: with a clear set of goals oriented toward customer expectations and incentives aligned to encourage desirable behavior, an organization can embrace change and reap the rewards of a culture of continuous learning and improvement, a culture in which everyone understands what needs to be done and embraces their role in the ongoing process of learning and optimizing.

What was the last change you feared in your workplace? When it was completed, was it good or bad?

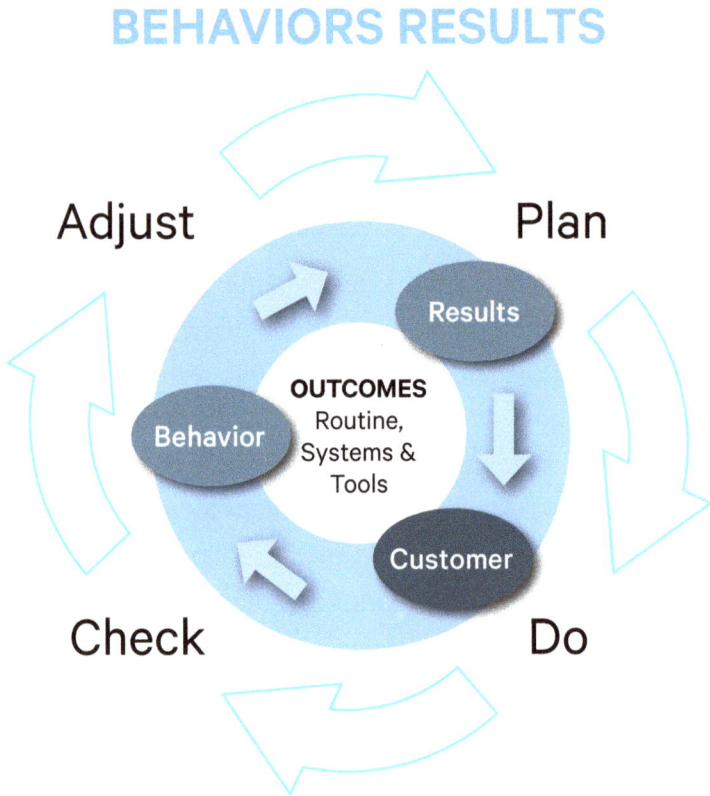

Figure 1.2—Outward circle (©Action New Thinking)

In concluding this chapter, we reflect on some of these questions before moving on to the next chapter:

- Have you defined your desired behaviors that drive sustainable results?
- How do they vary at different levels of the organization?
- Have you thought about how you measure and recognize these ideal behaviors?

2

The Inward Circle

In the previous chapter, we addressed the outward circle of enterprise excellence, which is oriented toward the creation of better results to serve customers (Plenert, 2021). We saw how optimizing for better outcomes in terms of routines, systems, and tools can lead to optimization that better aligns results with customers. Now that we have addressed this outward circle of enterprise excellence, we can address its counterpart, the inward circle or inward circle of enterprise excellence.

Both the external and inward circles of enterprise excellence are designed to facilitate excellence—they are ways of thinking about excellence— and each is complementary to the other. Where the outward circle of enterprise excellence focuses on the connection between behavior, results, and customer satisfaction, the inward circle is focused on the connection between beliefs, thoughts, and behavior. The outward circle revolves around outcomes, while the inward circle revolves around mindsets. Neither is more critical than the other, and a company seeking excellence should pursue both simultaneously. The more a company can cultivate the outward circle—the connection between behavior, results, and customer desires—the better positioned it will be to cultivate the inward circle, turning beliefs into thoughts into behavior.

No doubt you've noticed something significant: the common element typical of each circle is behavior. And no small wonder: behavior is important for making sense of both outcomes, as per the outward circle, and mindsets, as per the inward circle. As we will see, we can integrate the two circles to create a model of enterprise excellence, uniting mindsets, behaviors, and results, connecting our own inner beliefs and values to the outcomes our companies produce for customers.

Plenert (2021) describes a case involving a factory that produced electroluminescent electronics—of the type used to light up, blink, and produce programmed effects on car and truck dashboard displays, as well as signage in grocery stores and casinos. The company had a more than 13% defect rate, which they compensated for by overproducing. This led to financial losses that affected their profitability. This is an obvious candidate for the outward wheel, but what about the inward wheel? As we will see, both are highly relevant. He was initially concerned with the lack of direction within the organization: without a coherent strategy, vision, and mission statement, the organization had nothing to give its focus, and there were no valid metrics by which to measure the strategic focus of any changes the organization made. To fix these problems, the author started with a strategy workshop, which all senior management had to attend. The workshop was to fix the organization's problems regarding the lack of principles, goals, vision, mission, etc. Plenert (2021) followed this with improvements designed to address new product development, measuring performance, tool training, and teaching everyone to be responsible for quality. About five months into the organizational transformation, the author had the factory shut down and gave the employees complete freedom to move things, fix things, and position anything anywhere in the plant—the only stipulation being that they could not produce a bad or defective part.

The effect of this experiment was worth mentioning because it shows something important about the power of the inward wheel in action. On the first day, there was no output, but the employees made an incredible, uncountable number of changes. On the second day, a few products were produced, and on the third day, the employees hit about 50% of normal output. But a funny thing happened on the fourth and fifth days: the employees exceeded normal output.

The reason for this change was that the author had successfully transformed the culture and, more precisely, the thoughts and beliefs of the people involved in the culture. Employees felt trusted by management, and this made them feel empowered. Their belief that they were trusted factored into a thought process in which they were empowered, and this led to changes in behavior—and all of this, collectively, can be said to describe a shift in mindset, highlighting the importance of the experience people go through to change their beliefs and behaviors.

As Plenert (2021) explained, the key thing here was that the changes were lasting: the organization let employees fix things that needed fixing within the plant. If they needed to make a change that required funding, they had only to make a compelling case to their manager, and the result was that the organization became characterized by reasonable funding for improvements. The ultimate outcomes of these inward circle transformations had positive ramifications for the outward circle: instead of overproducing and losing money, the factory experienced about a 20% increase in capacity because they did not waste as much time producing defective parts or fixing product failures. By the eighth month, the rate of defects was below 2%, and after 12 months, it was less than 1% (Plenert, 2021).

In keeping with the lessons we have learned, one of the key takeaways from this scenario is the connection between changing behaviors and changing results. After working to instill in management and employees the importance of vision, mission, and quality, Plenert (2021) changed the culture by changing the behaviors. Because he had worked on changing people's mindsets, he set them free to change the environment of the organization itself and produce better results—and crucially, the author did this by empowering the people who were best equipped to understand the problems affecting production and performance on the front line, namely the employees.

To give another similar example, Jones et al. (2023) described a situation in which one of the authors was asked for guidance by a Malaysian plant that rebuilt alternators and starters for the United States automobile market. The plant manager had a problem: as he explained, his competition down the street had a similar number of employees doing the same work, but the output was three times that of his plant. He was convinced that his employees were working as hard as his competition, so he did not think the issue was with their efforts. What was the problem? What could account for the discrepancy?

The answer came when they toured the production floor and did a "go and observe" exercise. The author took the plant manager to a specific workstation and asked the manager to observe how long the employee spent working on the product in proportion to how much time they spent moving the product around, doing setup, and then doing cleanup and other tasks. This exercise was designed to highlight the difference between value-adding versus non-value-adding time and the associated concept of waste. The results were illuminating for the plant manager, who realized that although his employees were indeed working hard, they were mostly doing busy work. He needs to reorganize their work so they create value and spend less time working on non-value-adding activities.

The question then became: Who should lead the effort to reorganize employees' work? The plant manager hit on the answer himself after a few seconds: the employees themselves should reorganize their work since they are the ones actually doing it. However, this plant was characterized by so much inefficiency that a basic understanding of tools was important, and the author had to teach them many things before they could get off the ground. However, the plant manager had internalized the key insight: the people best equipped to make improvements were the employees because they were on the ground executing the actual work (Jones et al., 2023).

Trusting employees to reorganize their work shows the core of the philosophy of continuous improvement: with the right training, support, encouragement, and incentives, employees can be trusted to help make sweeping changes that will improve the functioning and output of an organization. Putting this philosophy into practice requires bridging the gap between employees and management and the old ways of thinking about things that depict the relationship between the two as a simple chain of command. If employees are not simply subordinates tasked with carrying out management commands but actors and trusted change partners, the organization can reap massive benefits from a much more cohesive, united, and motivated employee base.

At the same time, even as organizations need to bridge the divide between employees and management, they also need to incorporate the efforts of different departments and agents within a department. As Jones et al. (2023) explained, most attempts to improve traditional department quality, engineering, information technology, and other departments are described in terms of lean, sigma, and agile. However, most attempts to improve human resource management, health and safety, and organizational development departments are characterized in terms of employee development, culture initiatives, and leadership improvement. The problem is that this division is artificial, and a commitment to continuous improvement requires us to transcend it (Jones et al., 2023).

Dividing the departments of an organization may seem to make good sense, but the problem becomes clear when one considers how this divisional approach produces contradictions. The goals of lean and other similar programs work well in terms of improving quality and IT departments. However, employee development, culture initiatives, and leadership improvement often have very different goals. This divided approach produces what Jones et al. (2023) call the disconnected bridge. Moving past this approach requires a rethinking of fundamentals: organizations must accept the need to move from a tool-based approach to a systematic approach, one that can integrate the more "things"-based departments (quality control, IT, etc.) with the more "people"-based departments (HR, health and safety, occupational development, etc.) (Jones et al., 2023).

An imperative thing to understand here is that the core problem with tool-based approaches is not that the tools are bad or deficient; rather, the problem is with how the tools are applied in a tool-oriented approach. Organizations take a tool and apply it at several levels, eventually creating an entire system around various levels. Similarly, people-based change management is too often consumed with communication. A sound plan for communication, one that is varied and situational, is a vitally important part of a change management strategy, but there is a much bigger picture in which the plan is only one tool. The whole cannot and should not be defined by the part: a change management strategy should include such parts as coaching, mentoring, active listening, measurement, analysis, etc., and each of these should use various tools. By transcending the divide imposed by the disconnected bridge, the organization can bring balance to its change management efforts and develop a capacity for continuous improvement (Jones et al., 2023).

Everything we have discussed so far is concerned with mindset or with the lens through which we see the world and our place in it. This includes work, relationships with others, and how our activities impact the world. The problems we have been discussing are all good examples of errors in mindset: too often, organizations have problems, inefficiencies, conflicts, and sub-optimal solutions because they have adopted a quick-fix behavioral band-aid approach to solving problems. The correction to this is to recognize the underlying mindset at the heart of the challenges and adopt a different, far more productive mindset.

What is this different, more productive mindset? The answer can be found in The Arbing Institute's (2016) book *The Outward Mindset*, which describes precisely the outward mindset (thus the title) one needs to adopt to do change management initiatives effectively. This mindset is characterized by a focus on the goals of the organization and the results, and it is a holistic mindset because it seeks to determine these for the organization. The outward mindset attempts to be helpful and responsible and make a real impact on the organization and the people who work there. It seeks to help individuals understand how they might be creating obstacles for other people's work, and it helps them to change how they work and relate to others in a way that leads to real and sustainable results.

How do you know the outward mindset when you see it? The Arbinger Institute (2016) introduces the idea by asking the reader to consider certain people in one's life. First, they ask one to think about the three people in one's life whom one likes the most. Think about who these people are. Maybe a spouse? A child? Second, they ask one to consider the two people who have had the most positive influence on one. They also ask the reader to consider their best boss, the person who inspires them to do their best, their three favorite co-workers, and the acquaintance they most respect.

Now, think about all of these people. Perhaps there is some overlap between the categories. Maybe one's three favorite people include one of the two people who have had the most influence on one, for example. Or maybe one's best boss also inspires one to do his best. The point of the exercise is what these people probably all have in common. If you are like most people, you probably chose the people in these categories because you feel seen by them. Something about how they interact with you convinces you they understand you, convinces you that you matter, and no doubt this feeling is based on reality: you feel you matter to them because you do matter to them.

With this in mind, what can we learn about mindsets? People who make you feel seen and feel as if you matter are generally good examples of an outward mindset. They show you that you matter to them. The manner in which they communicate with you shows they actually care about you— and this is the definition of the outward mindset. People who have an inward mindset are self-absorbed and show little or no regard for others.

But people with an outward mindset engage with others and show them they matter.

Understand this difference, and you will understand the universal key to effective change management: show people they matter to you, and you can motivate them to show extraordinary performance. When people believe they matter, they are more likely to give you their best and become capable of extraordinary feats of collaboration and innovation that one would not have believed were possible. And the great news is that the more one applies the outward mindset, the more one learns from those who show it, the better one can become at it, and the more one can become like the people one admires. How would you like to be more like the people you admire most? Take the time to perfect your outward mindset, and you're certain to be closer.

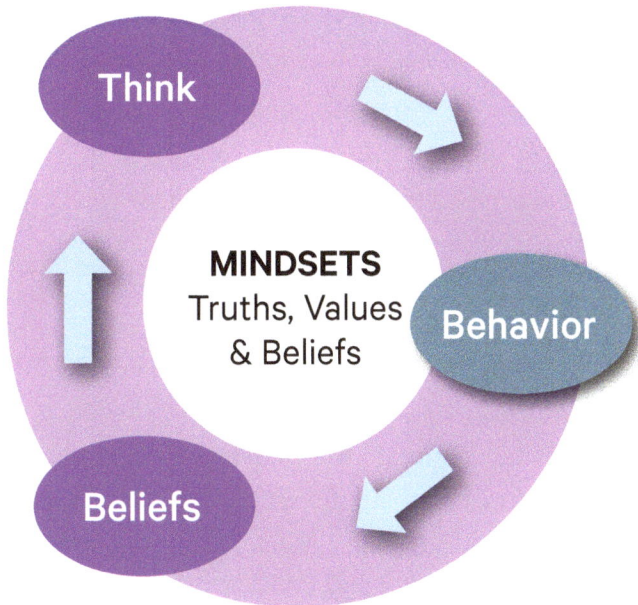

Figure 2.2—Inner circle (©Action New Thinking)

Then, developing our mindsets and training them toward an outward mindset is about learning how to see beyond ourselves. Figure 2.1 summarizes the inner circle or inner mindset. According to Paul Hubbard, CEO of a healthcare company, the reason so many leaders fail is that they step into a leadership role with a mandate. This is because they have a vision, and they tell others to do what they see. The problem is not that such leaders have a mission or a context but that they fail to help people see that. When people see what needs to be done—what can be improved and set right, and why, and how they can help—then they are more likely to put forth a heroic effort because they will have a sense of ownership of their work, crucially, when people not only *see* what needs to be done but also *do* it, they are motivated and capable of putting forth great effort— and they can be flexible and adapt to changing circumstances.

Thus, mindset lies at the very heart, the very foundation of everything we do: mindset determines so much how we engage with other people and how we behave, not only at work but in every situation. Mindset is everywhere, all the time, and if one can understand that and learn how to harness the outward mindset, great things will become possible. Conquer the challenges of mindset, and you will be well on your way to implementing an effective change management program. As we will see, mindset has a powerful impact on behavior: for better or worse, good or ill, it shapes everything we do.

However, focusing on mindset means pushing back against other, behaviorally oriented approaches to understanding results. To say that mindset is the foundation, that mindset is what drives results, is to say that one cannot simply focus on behavior—one cannot or should not simply incentivize desirable behavior and disincentivize undesirable behavior. How do we know that the behavioral approach is not the correct one? In a real sense, behaviors drive results: the behavior one engages in will determine the results one gets. If one engages in some simple task—folding laundry, say, or mowing the lawn—one will get predictable results (folded laundry, a fresh-mowed lawn). Why not focus on behavior? In fact, there are two very significant problems with behavior-driven approaches, and once we understand them, we will be more clearly able to see how important mindset is.

The first reason not to adopt the behavioral approach to results is that the behaviors people choose to engage in will depend on how they understand their situation. This will depend on the people with whom they interact. To return to the two simple examples referenced above, why does one choose to fold laundry? It may be because folding the laundry makes it easier to put away—but why does that matter? Folding the laundry is a thing one does because one believes it makes one's life better. For example, having neatly folded laundry in a predictable place reduces clutter and ensures one's clean clothes are where one wants them to be. Similarly, one mows the lawn because one believes that mowing the lawn will yield a better experience: a mowed lawn is more pleasant to look at and maybe more enjoyable to walk upon as well. For any behavior one engages in, mindset is relevant. Our mindsets determine everything we do.

The second reason is related to the first: mindset is present in one's behavior. Think about someone neat. How will they fold laundry? Maybe they will fold it neatly and carefully, and they will sort the different articles of clothing by type: socks, shirts, etc. Someone who does not value neatness might fold the laundry reluctantly and with less care. No doubt you have experienced such differences in performance in various workplaces. Think of a workplace task where you can remember different people performing with differing levels of enthusiasm and ability. Did people's attitudes come through in how well they performed the task?

I can remember a job in my youth in which I bagged groceries at a supermarket. Bagging groceries is a simple task, but one's level of enthusiasm and cheerfulness can powerfully affect one's self-presentation and engagement with the customer. Like many of my coworkers, I was cheerful, upbeat, and engaged—but other coworkers were less so. Even regarding very simple tasks, people's levels of care and enthusiasm can powerfully affect how they perform them.

It is also true that other people notice behavior and mindsets. Think about how powerful this can be: the levels of care and enthusiasm employees display in their work will usually have an impact on other employees and customers. No doubt we have all experienced very different levels of service when, for example, dining out. I can recall many instances in which I received professional, friendly, courteous service from servers. While my good experiences have far outnumbered the bad, I have also experienced sullen, resentful service. The difference is much more than a question of how long one must wait for food or a refill of a drink: when someone is committed to their work, there is ebullience, an enthusiasm impossible to miss. A friendly, cheerful server sends the message that you, the customer, matter. This makes all the difference in the dining experience—and that is the power of an outward mindset.

With this in mind, it should be easy to see the inherent problem with trying to make change by simply targeting behavior. If you only target behavior, you are not targeting mindset. Telling your employees, "Do this, not that," is not nearly as powerful as taking the time to make them feel they matter. This is done by communicating to them the reason they should do X instead of Y—and helping them develop the outward mindset of wanting to do exactly that. As Arbinger Institute (2016) explains, studies conducted by McKinsey & Company have found that organizations that focus on pervasive mindsets at first, at the outset, are four times more likely to succeed in their efforts to change their organizations. This is compared to companies that overlook this stage.

And the wonderful thing, too, about focusing on mindset is that it is actually much simpler than focusing on behavior. Instead of spelling out every little detail, every specific thing one is supposed to do or not do, one can help people understand the underlying reasons for doing something. The more people understand these underlying reasons. The easier it is to implement the desired changes because you will not have to spell out every part of everything: you will have people who understand the direction the company needs to go and who will be empowered to make many small changes and course corrections as your company implements much-needed changes. Even where you still have to stipulate specific behaviors, you will find far less resistance. After all, everyone will understand the reasons, and it will be much easier to convince.

And, too, you're likely to find that the more you cultivate an outward mindset, the more your people will think and act in ways that neither you nor any of them would have even imagined to be possible. Together, you will all go much farther and do a great deal more than anyone would have ever imagined before implementing an outward mindset. The reason for this, again, is that the outward mindset helps us to take account of others, and this helps us to take account of everything we do—because, after all, everything we do and everything we do does not have some effect on others.

We have so far treated the inward mindset—self-, inward-looking—and the outward mindset, which is outward-looking and other-focused-as binary. You are one or the other, and nothing in between. While this was a useful simplification to introduce the core concept, in reality, people and organizations usually exist on a spectrum, a continuum, between the two poles: the pure inward mindset on one end and the pure outward mindset on the other. No doubt you will not be surprised to consider that essentially any organization will be somewhere on the continuum but not at either end: even a dysfunctional organization is unlikely to have an inward mindset, with no regard for others' feelings and concerns, and even a high-functional organization is likely to be subject to some inward mindset blind-spots. With the continuum in mind, however, we can consider how best to move people from the more inward-mindset- part of the continuum toward the polestar of the outward mindset—and we want to do that because it is the foundation of all accountability, collaboration, innovation, leadership, culture, and value to customers.

The core of the outward mindset, as we have seen, is being attuned to and caring about other people's needs, goals, interests, and challenges. People with an outward mindset see other people as people. The inward mindset sees people not as people but as objects who may either help or hinder one in the pursuit of one's own goals: those who help are vehicles, while those who hinder are obstacles. Crucially, one should not confuse the inward mindset with introspection since introspection can help cultivate self-knowledge and help one be more mindful and considerate of others.

One very important and valuable way to understand the difference between these two mindsets, and the reason that the outward mindset is so superior to the inward mindset, is that the outward mindset is actually the truth. Other people are more than vehicles to help us reach our goals or obstacles in the way: they are people, and they have their own goals, goals, and desires. Once one understands this clearly, one can move forward in a way that is more effective than if one is stuck in an inward mindset, trying to figure out who will help one with one's goals and who will hinder them. Caring about people is the precondition to improving performance—after all, who are we performing for, if not other people?

Our organizations produce goods and services for customers, so we need to consider them. And if we want to improve what we do, we need to consider employees' well-being, goals, and objectives.

Having acknowledged the advantages of the outward mindset, we must confront an important question at the heart not only of business but all of human behavior: if it is so useful and good to have an outward mindset, why then does anyone indulge in the inward mindset? Why would anyone adopt this damaging, false, self-limiting view of the world? The answer lies in human behavior and the challenging nature of the world. We are fallible, and we inevitably get in our own way—and sometimes, there are understandable reasons for this.

To better understand this dynamic, take a moment to think about someone difficult you once worked with. No doubt we have all been there: we have all had a lazy coworker, shirked their duties, curried favor with the boss in manipulative ways, and so on. There are numerous ways people can be difficult to work with. They might have annoying personal habits, be personally unpleasant, pay little attention, and leave one to do the most onerous work. And this is to say nothing of *bosses*. Who was your worst boss ever? What was working for them like? We have all had a boss who was unpleasant, uncourteous, unreasonable and demanding.

Framing it like this, it becomes easier to see how one might view these people as annoying obstacles to one's best interests, if not the bane of one's existence. Maybe the behavior of these people leads us to build up a mental model of them as lazy, uncooperative, unpleasant, etc. I know that when I think of my least favorite coworkers in my work history, the associations that come to mind are not flattering. Similarly, when I think of my worst boss, the picture is not a good one. Thinking about these people, I understand well how someone might not wish to cooperate with coworkers or their boss.

And now, we understand the inward mindset. It is a human thing to do when we do not like our experiences with someone; we see them in ways that sustain the negative picture we have of them. Think of one of your least favorite coworkers from an earlier job: if you discovered a piece of information about the company that would help you and them, would you be inclined to share it with them? From the outward mindset, the answer should be yes: even if you do not like the person, you should want to help them because their success is tied to yours, given you work for the same organization. However, if you have a negative, limiting view of that person, it will be easy to say you should not share information. Given your experiences with them, it feels justified—but therein lies the trap of an inward mindset.

As with human follies generally, the inward mindset is not simply something for bad or selfish people: it is a human failing, and even the best of us will succumb to it. We all have limited time, energy, and patience. If someone pushes our buttons repeatedly, we run out of patience and are less likely to want to see them as our coworker who has shared interests in the success of the company: we are more likely to, in some sense, dehumanize them and see them simply as an obstacle to our goal of a good and harmonious work experience. And with this in view, should we not minimize our interactions with them? The problem, though, is that when we burn time and energy justifying our response to them, a response that will generally waste that time and energy creating a silo to insulate ourselves from that person—and if that mindset catches on in an organization, the results can be bad.

Everyone inevitably succumbs to the temptations of the inward mindset. However, the cure lies in realizing that when we do this, we are getting in our own way: we are allowing ourselves to burn time and energy justifying our treatment of others as obstacles instead of trying to connect with them and help to create positive-sum results for everyone. When we cultivate an outward mindset, we do not shy from the challenge of making common connections and causes with others, even and especially the ones we find difficult. This is how we grow, both as individuals and as an organization: not by avoiding problems but by confronting them and productively and proactively engaging with them.

The power of this outward- mindset is precisely that it is an other- mindset. We are looking at others not as obstacles or vehicles but rather with an eye toward their needs, objectives, and challenges. We are focused not on our own goals alone but rather on shared goals. We are asking ourselves not "What can I achieve?" but instead, "What can we achieve together?" Doing this and adopting this mindset is powerful because it is something that people pick up on, something that motivates people to want to help us accomplish great things together.

What does this look like in action? Let us consider the unlikely example of Bill Bartmann, founder and CEO of a company called CFS2... a debt collection company. For many people, the words "debt collectors" conjure up negative associations, and with good reason—but Bill wanted to create a debt collection company that was different, a debt collection company founded on treating debtors with respect. As a person who has known his own share of hard financial times, Bill understands that the reason people do not pay back the money they have borrowed is precisely because they do not have the money they owe. By adopting an outward mindset, Bill reframed the challenge: instead of seeking to browbeat debtors and squeeze whatever he could out of them, he started by thinking about who they were and what their situations were.

By taking this approach, Bill and his people radically changed the paradigm of debt collection: instead of seeking to squeeze their clients, they set about trying to figure out how to help them make money. At first, Bill tried asking his workforce to brainstorm and experiment to see how they could help their clients get jobs, and his employees tried helping the clients by giving them advice and suggestions about what to do. However, they soon ran into a problem, as summarized by one of Bill's employees: the clients were so beaten down that they could not "get up and go" and were unable or unwilling to do the heavy lifting themselves.

Rather than abandoning his attempts to do good and help his clients, Bill and his employees doubled down: they started writing résumés for their clients. They also looked for job opportunities, helped clients fill out applications, and scheduled job interviews. They even took it upon themselves to run mock interviews to prepare clients for the real thing. They even started calling their clients in the mornings of their appointments to get them out of bed early enough to arrive at the interviews on time. After that, they found other ways to help: any headache in their clients' lives meant an opportunity to help. They identified organizations dedicated to helping those in need and worked to partner with those organizations to meet their clients' needs. Best of all, they did this at no extra cost to the client—Bill structures his employees' compensation not based on how much debt they collect but rather on how many free services they can provide for their clients.

On the surface, this sounds too good to be true. How can a debt collection company work this way, providing extensive handholding customized to individual debtors and still turn a profit? And yet, the results speak for themselves: after three years of debt collection, CSF2's collection rate was twice that of any other firm in the debt collection industry. This is the power of the outward mindset: it takes difficult interpersonal and organizational challenges and works to find opportunities based on people's needs.

How does one move from the inward mindset to the outward mindset? There is a helpful formula called SAM, which consists of three steps: **See** others, **Adjust** efforts, and **Measure** impact. For a good example of this formula in action, consider Alan Mulally, who Ford Motor Company hired as president and CEO in September 2006. Ford was bleeding $17 billion per year, and they decided to bet the farm on Mulally as their last best hope. Mulally soon discovered that no one at Ford felt responsible for the many problems that beset the company—and so he set about to change the underlying mindset by taking people's needs into account. First, he used a mechanism for weekly meetings called the Business Plan Review, or BPR. He trained the members of his executive team to come to meetings prepared with charts that documented the performance of their areas of responsibility and that compared the outcomes with the company's plan. He also had them color-code the items on the charts: items going according to plan were colored green, while items at risk of going off plan were colored yellow, and items off plan were colored red.

Additionally, Mulally introduced 10 BPR rules designed to focus everyone on centering people while providing a compelling vision. At first, all the executives brought all-green charts... but the reason for this was that Ford's company culture demanded that executives not be wrong. If an executive were wrong, they would lose their position. This came to a head for Mark Fields, responsible for Ford's operations in the Americas, just before the new Ford Edge was to be shipped out of Oakville, Ontario, in Canada: a test driver found that the tailgate on one of the test vehicles had an actuator problem. This put Fields in a difficult position: if he sat on the report and the vehicles turned out to be faulty, he would lose his job—but if he told the truth up front, he was gone.

After thinking it over, Fields decided to tell the truth. He came to the meeting with a solid red chart and told everyone that the Ford Edge might have a problem. But instead of firing Fields, Mulally smiled and applauded him. Fields asked the other executives for help. The spell was broken: another executive said that he had seen the issue on another vehicle and would get Fields those results. Another offered to get his top-flight engineers to Oakville to help with any needed redesign.

The rest of the story is well-known and easily told. Mulally shepherded his executives through working on the Edge. Along the way, he helped to instill a new culture of honesty, accountability, and collaboration in the company. The experiences the executives had from this revised behavior from Mulally changed the executives' beliefs. Thus, their behaviors now work out of their silos and work collectively as one connected team. Ford was able to right its fortunes, pulling itself out in front of the financial crisis of 2007-2008—it was the only American auto manufacturer who did not have to take a federal bailout to survive. Mulally helmed Ford until his retirement in 2014—when Mark Fields replaced him. This is the power of the outward mindset: by cultivating an other- mindset, a company can replace a toxic, counter-productive corporate culture with a helpful, collaborative, and far more competitive one.

What lessons can we take from the example of the Ford turnaround? Let's break it down into the three elements of the outward mindset pattern. The first step concerns seeing the needs, objectives, and challenges of others— and that is what Mulally did with the BPR process. He accomplished this process by providing the members of his team with insight into their contributions, and at the same time, he helped them understand the needs, goals, challenges, and activities of their colleagues. Mulally himself had an outward mindset in the way that he worked with his team and conducted the meetings, and that helped him create a forum for change by helping everyone see how their roles in the organization related to everyone else and their roles.

After Mulally had helped his team to see the challenges they all faced, he could take them to the second step of the outward mindset pattern, namely adjusting their work to be more helpful to others. We saw this regarding Mark Fields: Mulally was happy to ask other team members to step forward and help Mark with the Ford Edge issue. The reason for this was that he wanted them to take responsibility not only for themselves but also for how they affected others.

With these two important steps accomplished, Mulally could lead his team to the third and final part of the process. The team gathered together to see if what they were doing to help was actually helping, actually making an impact and improving results. Measuring impact is the third step, and it is crucial because it provides information and feedback that can be used to tailor future efforts. Without measuring results, we have no way of knowing if what we are doing is working. Measure the results consistently and well, and you have a powerful stream of information providing insights into whether your efforts are translating into effective outcomes. In addition, you can see what areas could still use improvement.

Summary

The ultimate lesson of the outward mindset is taking responsibility, not only for oneself but for others. What we must learn if we are to apply the outward mindset correctly is that other people in our organization are not our rivals or our foes—rather, it is our selfishness and short-sightedness that we must vanquish. The inward mindset, the outlook that views everything in terms of "How is this good for me and my goals?" is a quintessential human failing—and though it is altogether understandable, it is still something we must overcome if we are to make the most of our resources and inaugurate a culture of accountability, innovation, dynamism, and continuous improvement. By taking responsibility for not only us but also how our actions impact others, we can take important steps toward the building of a new and collaborative culture in our organizations. By mastering this outward mindset, we can propel our organizations to a state of continuous improvement.

The inward circle of enterprise excellence concerns the connection between beliefs, thoughts, and behavior and how these things revolve around mindsets. As we have seen in this chapter, that is the key to its power: the inward circle is how companies turn beliefs into thoughts into behaviors, a formulation that can be powerful when applied well. When employees believe management trusts them, as in the example with the factory that produces electroluminescent electronics, they feel sufficiently empowered, as in the example, to make the decisions they need to make to improve processes—or to improve productivity within the company otherwise. Belief is an enormously powerful thing, and it can be used for good or for ill: you are likely to find that a key aspect of dysfunctional or suboptimal behaviors in your organization pertains to beliefs, to what people think is expected of them. As we have seen repeatedly in this chapter, it is often the employees themselves who are the best and most important asset in the rollout of continuous improvement initiatives: that they understand their work and the problems about it means they are likely to provide invaluable input regarding reforming it, as necessary. Taking this approach is also likely to help your employees believe that they matter, and as we have seen, this belief is an extraordinarily powerful and important one: when people believe that they matter, they usually act like it, and that means showing extraordinary performance.

In concluding this chapter, we reflect on some of these questions before moving on to the next chapter:

- Are you aware of your personal values?
- Are you aware of your personal beliefs? If not, how could you help articulate them?
- Are you aware of your team's conscious and subconscious values and beliefs?
- Do the team's values align with the organization's charter values?

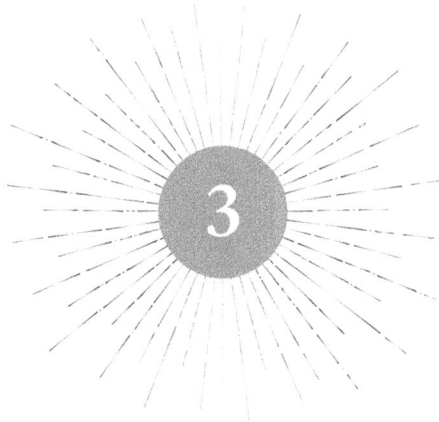

The Mindset Framework— Bringing the Two Circles Together

What is the connection between outcomes and mindsets? In the first chapter, we saw how the outward circle of enterprise excellence linked behavior, results, and customer satisfaction to create better outcomes. This was done with outcomes being the central "hub" around which the outward circle, or wheel, revolves. In the second chapter, we saw how beliefs, thoughts, and behavior are linked in an inward circle that revolves around mindsets. We also learned that neither circle is more important than the other, and cultivating the outer outward circle will help a company cultivate the inward circle as well. A company that masters both circles will likely reach new heights of excellence, and now that we've covered each circle separately, it's time to look at how we bring them together.

The general process or conceptual model is easy to summarize, so let's cover it now. Your overall strategy should be to **start with the outward circle**, and as you improve and become more proficient, your behaviors become better and more excellent. Now, here's the connection with the inward circle: as the behaviors improve, and you continue to affirm the improved behaviors, your organization should be able to build on or challenge current beliefs and alignment with personal and organizational values and evolve employee thinking until the behaviors become unconscious habits. Once a behavior becomes a habit, your employees and your organization will perform it reflexively and without giving it a lot of thought—and that's a good thing, so long as the habits are desirable ones.

Now, why start with the outward circle and then link to the inward circle, as opposed to the other way around? If you think about Simon Sinek's "Start with Why," you would think it would be logical to do it the other way around. In the planning stage, when figuring out how to use the model, absolutely start with your overall purpose, behaviors, and underlying beliefs. However, the key thing is not to push the beliefs first: you want to change people's behaviors and incentivize the desired behaviors, and then—and only then—will it be time to introduce beliefs to help reinforce the behaviors. Once you are affirming behaviors and encouraging employees to change their beliefs about the operation of the company toward the new system, you'll be well on your way to establishing changed habits.

But why habits? What's so important about habits? We all know that some habits can be undesirable or destructive, but they are behaviors people do reflexively and without deliberative behavior. Can habits make such a profound impact? The answer is yes, and the change may surprise you.

Let's take a look at one story about using behavior to change lots of little habits. This one is from the world of British Cycling, the governing body for professional cycling in Great Britain. In 2003, the organization hired Dave Brailsford as its new performance director and tasked him with the monumental challenge of giving the sport an overhaul (Clear, 2018). While it may be hard to believe now, at the time, British cycling had endured nearly a century-long run of underwhelming mediocrity: only one Olympic gold medal since 1908 and no wins in the Tour de France in 110 years. The situation was so bad that one of Europe's top bike manufacturers refused to sell their bikes to the British because they were afraid it would damage their image and hurt sales. What was Brailsford to do?

Brailsford employed an entire strategy: a relentless, unswerving commitment to what he called "the aggregation of marginal gains." The core idea was simple: for each and everything you do, look for a way to do it just a little, tiny bit better. Brailsford thought that if British cyclists could take each and every aspect of riding a bike and improve it by a mere 1 percent, the cumulative results would be significant. In keeping with this philosophy, Brailsford and his coaches rolled out an array of small adjustments that were perfectly in aligning with the kinds of things any cycling team would do to try to get better: redesigned bike seats for greater comfort, alcohol rubbed on the tires for a better grip; electrically heated over shorts for ideal muscle temperature; testing of various fabrics in a wind tunnel, and so on (Clear, 2018).

However, Brailsford and his team kept going, and before long, they had found a little improvement of 1 percent in overlooked and unexpected areas. The examples ranged from testing different kinds of massage gels to find which one produced the fastest muscle recovery to the type of pillow and mattress that led to the best night's sleep for each rider. They even produced the idea of painting the inside of the truck white, which made it easier to spot even small bits of dust—after all, dust could degrade the performance of bikes, and dust spotted could be cleaned up (Clear, 2018).

What was the outcome of all of these little improvements? The results were staggering: the team dominated the road and track cycling events at the 2008 Olympic Games in Beijing, winning 60 percent of the gold medals available. And four years later, in their own capital of London, the British outdid themselves again: they set nine Olympic records and seven world records. Within the same year, Bradley Wiggins became the first British cyclist to win the Tour de France. Their teammate Chris Froome won it the next year, and he went on to win it again in the years of 2015, 2016, and 2017 (Clear, 2018).

The key lesson of British cycling is this: improve performance in lots of little ways, with lots of little habits, and you can get huge results. In fact, if you zero in on what people need to believe in doing a behavior consistently, the habit can become embedded, and all the automatic thinking is pushed into the subconscious. As it turns out, an excellent place to start is with a keystone habit: a habit that drives changes toward productivity and improvement in many different areas of an organization or an individual's life.

Alcoa, the Aluminum Company of America, is a company with a long and distinguished history: the company's founder, Charles Martin Hall, invented the process of smelting aluminum. But by 1987, the company was running into trouble, thanks to rising competition and unwise attempts to expand into new product lines. Alcoa's board of directors announced that there would be a change of leadership, much to investors' relief, but their choice was Paul O'Neill, a government bureaucrat with little reputation on Wall Street (Duhigg, 2012).

O'Neill made quite the splash at a meet-and-greet in a Manhattan ballroom when he opened his mouth and said he wanted to talk about worker safety. He acknowledged that Alcoa's safety record was better than the general American workforce, particularly in light of the fact that their employees worked with molten metals and dangerous machines, but he said that wasn't good enough. What O'Neill wanted was a workplace with zero injuries. It was a radical departure from the predictable formula for these events: O'Neil hadn't talked about taxes, regulations, right-sizing, or synergistic market advantage (Duhigg, 2012).

Investors were spooked: they thought O'Neill was a crazy hippie who was going to kill the company. Yet, within a year, O'Neill guided the company in recording high profits. By the time he retired in 2000, the company's annual net income was five times what it had been when he arrived, and its market capitalization was up by $27 billion. What is perhaps even more astonishing is that all of this growth happened while Alcoa became one of the safest companies in the world. Before O'Neill, it was common for most Alcoa plants to have at least one accident per week. After he implemented his safety plan, however, it was common enough for entire facilities to go for years without so much as one employee losing one workday due to an accident. The worker injury rate hit a mere one-twentieth of the US average (Duhigg, 2012).

The secret to this remarkable transformation was elegantly simple, and it all concerned O'Neill's audacious goal. To make change happen, he focused on keystone habits, habits that would dislodge and remake the company's patterns of behavior across the board. And by focusing on safety, Alcoa had to change lots of other things. It all started with O'Neill's approach, which focused on trying to understand why injuries happened in the first place (Duhigg, 2012).

During his time in the federal bureaucracy, O'Neill learned to ask why patterns were occurring and keep asking questions until he reached a root cause. To get to the root causes of injuries, O'Neill created a system designed to implement a habit loop: any time an injury occurred, the unit president had to report it to O'Neill within twenty-four hours and present a plan for ensuring the injury never happened again. Compliance with this program came with a reward: embracing the program was a prerequisite for getting promoted (Duhigg, 2012).

For a unit president to meet this requirement, however, they needed to hear about the accident from their vice presidents when the accident happened. This meant that vice presidents had to communicate with floor managers, and floor managers constantly needed to get workers to raise warnings quickly whenever they saw a problem. Floor managers needed workers to suggest safety improvements. This was so that any time a vice president asked for a plan, they would have a reservoir of them in an idea box. All of this meant that a long-established hierarchy within one of the largest companies on earth had to retool its communication systems so ideas could flow from the bottom to the top, from the workers on the ground floor all the way to O'Neill (Duhigg, 2012).

Starting with safety and creating a simple habit loop caused other changes within the company, solving longstanding problems. Labor unions at Alcoa had long opposed measuring individual workers' productivity, but they did a volte-face when they realized that such measurements could help determine circumstances under which the manufacturing process was going awry and posing a danger to workers. On the other hand, managers had long resisted giving workers autonomy to shut down a production line when the pace became overwhelming, but now they were happy to embrace this policy as a way to pre-empt injuries (Duhigg, 2012).

O'Neill never sold Alcoa on his safety regimen with the promise of increased profits, and yet, this is what happened. As O'Neill's program of safety worked its way through the organization, costs went down, quality went up, and productivity positively skyrocketed. And nothing about this was random or coincidental: by focusing on safety, Alcoa accomplished these other things. For example, pouring systems were redesigned to keep molten metal from injuring workers when it splashed. This led to fewer injuries, but it also saved money because of reduced spillage of raw materials. If a machine continued to break down, Alcoa replaced it, which meant less risk of injury for employees. It also meant higher-quality products, and the reason for this was, as Alcoa discovered, that equipment malfunctions were a leading cause of less-than-optimal aluminum (Duhigg, 2012).

The effects of focusing on safety are compounded thanks to the enhanced communication O'Neill promotes within the organization. He gave his phone number to the hourly workers, telling them that if their management did not follow up on safety issues, they should call him at home and talk to him personally. The phone began to ring, but the workers were less interested in talking about safety and more interested in sharing other ideas. For example, Alcoa plants manufactured aluminum siding. The executives of the plant would try to guess which colors would be popular, and they inevitably guessed wrong. This led to many situations in which the warehouses were overflowing with a color no one wanted, even as they were devoid of the in-demand colors. A low-level employee produced a brilliant solution: group all the painting machines together, letting the plant switch out the pigments faster and respond more quickly to changing consumer demand. The idea was so good that within a year, Alcoa's aluminum siding profits doubled (Duhigg, 2012).

O'Neill's work at Alcoa is a testament to the power of habit: by creating a habit loop, O'Neill trained an entire organization to make safety a habit. And over time, that keystone habit transformed the landscape of the organization in ways that made it more profitable and far, far safer. This attests to the power of habit, and it dovetails nicely with researcher Michael I. Norton's findings about the benefits of workplace rituals, benefits that are far-reaching (Norton, 2024).

It is obvious that the benefits of workplace habits are centered on safety, such as those we discussed regarding Alcoa. But what is one to make of other workplace rituals, such as the Wal-Mart cheer? For the uninitiated, the cheer starts with "Give me a W!" and spells out the name Wal-Mart before ending with "Whose Wal-Mart, is it? It's my Wal-Mart" (Norton, 2024). Rituals like this are easy to dismiss as silly and trivial, but Norton says they are anything but: his research points to rituals, including something as seemingly trivial as the Wal-Mart cheer, as vitally important for providing structure and meaning at work and for increasing involvement—and they seem to have many benefits (Norton, 2024).

Norton has distilled three major insights from his work, the first being that many rituals people report engaging in at work are not mandated by corporations but crafted by employees themselves. His second insight is that workplace rituals help to provide structure and meaning to a workday. Employees use them to start their days, perform them ahead of stressful meetings and presentations, rely on them in their teams, and even use them at the end of the workday. These rituals are nothing to be dismissed: Norton's third major insight is these rituals are often linked with actual benefits, including better work-life balance and better teamwork (Norton, 2024).

Norton studied nearly 140 participants, all recruited from Harvard Business Review readers. He found that 79% reported having a regular practice with which to start their day, with typical themes including prayer, meditation, exercise, and—unsurprisingly—coffee. As Norton explains, this is a common theme even with the most notable artists (Norton, 2024).

Norton's work points to the importance of rituals throughout the day. He found that 63% of his participants reported engaging in rituals before stressful meetings or presentations. They said they used specific types of preparation, deep breathing exercises, and music. This dovetails with work from researchers at Washington University in St. Louis, who posit these kinds of pre-performance rituals help alleviate stress by simply forcing people to focus on something besides the performance they are about to give, thus giving them less time and space to spiral out of control and panic. One response that embodies this comes from the participant who wrote:

"Breathe deeply and think of being a leaf that flies lightly" (Norton, 2024).

Team rituals seem less common, but 38% of Norton's sample reported engaging in them. Many of these rituals occurred during meetings, with the most common types centered on sharing good news, playing music, and engaging in breathing exercises. One example a participant gave was that of 90-second silent breathing exercises, which their team engaged in before internal team meetings conducted by Zoom. The silent breathing exercises helped them to settle into themselves and shift their presence to the specific meeting (Norton, 2024).

Dr. Morgan Jones

Another example of a team-oriented ritual was given by a participant who reported that staff meetings used an icebreaker. Specifically, they asked each member of the team to participate in bringing in an icebreaker, and they switched it off for each meeting. Icebreakers included everything from Two Truths and a Lie to "If this meeting were a song, which song would it be?" Doing this ritual helps the meeting start on a positive note. Similarly, another reader reported that for their team meetings, they shared positive developments, speaking both personally and professionally, and sometimes ended them by talking about what they were looking forward to regarding the weekends (Norton, 2024).

Another survey respondent noted that eating together helped bring teams together. They contrasted the teams that ate together with those where each member ate separately and noted that the teams who ate together seemed more connected. Norton (2024) indicated that his research seems to point to the importance of team rituals like these for bringing people together. He found that members of teams who reported having at least one ritual usually viewed their work as having more meaning than those teams who reported having no rituals at all (Norton, 2024).

In addition to using rituals to start workdays, gear up for presentations, build teamwork and break the ice in meetings, Norton's (2024) research found that employees usually use rituals to end their workdays as well. He noted that 59% of readers reported having a ritual to end their workday, with the most common being to shut off technology and create a space for transition before connecting with family (Norton, 2024).

For example, one reader said that closing all the open tabs and applications on their computer and shutting it down helped them mark the completion of one day and kept them from being "triggered" the next morning by seeing "unfinished" work from the day before. Another reader said that at the end of their workday, they looked to see whether anyone from their team was still online—and if so, they asked if the team member needed help or to encourage the team member to close up and enjoy their evening. This was followed by shutting down their laptop, turning off the office light, and closing the door behind them. The reader specifically explained that creating a separate office space and being able to close that door at the end of the day made it easier to separate from work once they were done for the day (Norton, 2024).

What should we make of these rituals? The main takeaway is that rituals are not meaningless: they tend to be both useful and effective and help us complete our workdays more successfully. Norton and his colleague Francesca Gino and their other colleagues have found that rituals play several critical roles in our lives: rituals we perform in the face of loss can help us to feel less grief, while rituals performed with family can make us feel closer. Rituals with our partners can reinforce our commitment to each other. They also noted that rituals do not have to be elaborate and ceremonial, i.e., they do not necessarily have to embody pomp and circumstance (Berinato, 2020).

Most rituals are private and idiosyncratic to the people who practice them. Think of holiday celebrations, such as Christmas or Thanksgiving in America: every family does it differently. This is a feature, not a bug: Norton and his colleagues think that the idiosyncrasy of these rituals can help people get the desired benefit out of them, i.e., connection and family togetherness. If your family has a specific, idiosyncratic way to celebrate Thanksgiving and Christmas—or another significant family holiday—then it is all the more special because it is unique to your family (Berinato, 2020).

With this in mind, how can we use idiosyncratic rituals to improve productivity and integrate inward and outward circles? The short answer is **belief**: if we harness the power of belief to the creation of good habits, we can get to a point at which we perform those habits automatically, with no special effort, precisely because of what we believe about the habit and ourselves. And there may be no better example than personal fitness.

Do you know anyone serious about fitness? I don't mean an Olympic athlete or bodybuilder; I mean anyone who works out multiple days a week and has been at it long enough to produce very notable results. A colleague of mine has a fitness regimen that extends over six days of the week, from Monday through Saturday, and she has heavily ritualized it. For example, on Monday, Wednesday, and Friday, she does calisthenics and weightlifting, which are always in the same sequence. Her rituals include not only the exercises but also the podcasts and YouTube videos she plays while working out. On Tuesdays and Thursdays, she does light calisthenics and runs, and on Saturdays, she skips the calisthenics and only runs.

What I can tell you is that fitness has changed her life: She has more energy, clearer thinking, and generally has a more positive outlook on life. Another interesting thing has happened over the past decade: her fitness routine has become more automatic. It still takes willpower—her combination burpee-mountain-climber is a grind, and it is one calisthenic exercise she does five days a week—but that willpower has become more automatic to where it would be harder for her to go a day without doing her scheduled exercise (not counting Sunday, which she always takes off).

Her commitment to fitness has helped her develop beliefs *about* fitness that are part of the process as well. Specifically, she **loves** fitness. She is passionate about staying in good shape and believes there is nothing better one can do for one's good health and longevity. She has seen the results of her fitness practice in an improved physique and state of mind. This makes me all the more committed to the routine.

Now, what's the connection between her fitness routine and the rest of this chapter, namely the integration of the outward and inward circles? Let's map it out, starting with the outward circle: her fitness behaviors led to results (she felt better and was in better shape), and as the "customer" of this practice, she experienced customer satisfaction (as noted) and better outcomes (she became more fit). Viewing outcomes as the hub, my outcomes were better fitness... and everything that comes with it, including better energy, mindset, etc.

Really, she can't stress enough how much fitness has changed her life, and that provides me with the perfect integration into the inward circle. Her beliefs about fitness, namely that it is good and desirable and leads to all kinds of better life outcomes, are connected to changes in her thoughts and behaviors. For example, she can still vividly remember how profoundly difficult it was to force herself to go on a run ten years ago. She found it very difficult, and she would spend much of her time fighting with herself, trying to put her mind over matter and make herself keep going even as her body screamed at her to stop.

Over time, though, it became easier, and eventually, she did not have to think as hard about doing my daily fitness routines—that is to say, it became more automatic. My thinking patterns switched from "I have to psych myself up to do this, and I have to force myself to put mind over matter" to "I'm really craving my run." This has been her experience with many of her more challenging routines, and even after she mastered running, she had similar experiences with a combination burpee-mountain-climber core exercise she performed. After about four years, though, she is at the point where she expects it, and she partly relies on it to wake me up. All this started when this friend asked me to coach her to go to the gym; the goal was never to go to the gym but to look at what going to the gym enabled her to do. We focused on her desire to ride horseback on a beach and build her core strength to do this bareback.

Once you reach this level, willpower becomes automatic, and your new and improved habits become things you perform automatically. Something that you might have once had to force yourself to do becomes pleasurable: your body learns to embrace the grind, and you develop beliefs about your habits that help you keep going and even build on what you are doing.

The beautiful thing is that once you learn this habit formation cycle—once you master the two wheels and can build positive habits to where your willpower becomes automatic through embedded beliefs — then you can apply this same basic process to building up more positive habits. For example, she found that her fitness practice has actually helped with her work: I'm far more disciplined and methodical than I ever was before I became serious about fitness. Master the outward circle-inward circle process of habit formation for continuous improvement, and the world is your oyster—with enough hard work.

You may be wondering if anyone has ever thought of applying insights like these for continuous improvement in organizations—and they have. One of the better examples is Starbucks. For the global coffee titan, willpower is a vital resource, and the company has spent incredible amounts of time and money cultivating and building up its employees (Duhigg, 2012).

Back in the late 1990s, when Starbucks was planning to undertake its massive growth expansion, company executives realized something very important: if they wanted to succeed on the scope and scale they planned, they needed to do more than sell lattes and scones. What they needed to do was create an environment that would justify paying, say, four dollars for a fancy cup of coffee. That meant the company needed to train its employees to give customers joy along with their lattes and scones—and here is where Starbucks made an incredible breakthrough (Duhigg, 2012).

Instead of merely establishing a set of company standards and designing a basic training curriculum, Starbucks started to research how to teach employees to regulate their emotions and marshal self-discipline so they could deliver a burst of pep with every serving. They realized that unless baristas can be trained to put aside personal problems, some employees will let their emotions spill over, which will have ugly effects on customer treatment and satisfaction. They spent millions of dollars on the alternative: creating curriculums to train employees on self-discipline. Starbucks executives wrote workbooks that serve as guides on how to make willpower a habit. And their curriculums have been so successful that they can take even people who come from troubled upbringings and broken homes—children of drug addicts, for example—and teach them the discipline and self-control needed to succeed. The key to the whole thing was a startling realization: willpower is like a muscle, and it can be augmented through practice (Duhigg, 2012).

Starbucks drew on some remarkable research on willpower, including the work of two Australian researchers, Megan Oaten and Ken Cheng. This duo wanted to test the idea that willpower was like a muscle, i.e., something that could be strengthened through exercise. To test the idea, they recruited two dozen people, ranging in age from eighteen to fifty. They put them through a two-month fitness program, subjecting them to more weightlifting, resistance training, and aerobic routines. When the experiment ended, they found that participants were not only in better physical shape—before the experiment, most were self-described couch potatoes—but they also showed greater willpower in other areas of their lives. They consumed less alcohol, caffeine, and tobacco and spent more hours on homework and fewer watching TV. In later experiments, Oaten and Cheng confirmed these results: the more willpower people build up through physical fitness, the more willpower they have in other areas of their lives, too (Duhigg, 2012).

Starbucks tried to leverage this research by getting employees into fitness, but attendance and results were spotty. But they kept working at the problem until they found a solution: make willpower a habit by teaching employees how to respond to specific cues, in particular, inflection points that would test their willpower to the breaking point—an angry, screaming customer or a long line at the cash register. Management drilled employees on specific routines and procedures, role-playing until responses became automatic. They also taught employees to recognize specific rewards—a grateful customer, praise from a manager—that they could look to for evidence that the job was well done. By choosing behaviors ahead of time, employees learned to follow specific routines in the face of pressure—and then, with time and practice, they made good on their habits. This is the power of integrating the outward and inward circles: the culmination of everything we have been discussing is the ability to work at the formation of positive habits until willpower becomes automatic (Duhigg, 2012).

Summary

Bringing the outward and inward circles together is the key to cultivating the mindset that lies at the heart of continuous improvement: the outward circle of behavior, results, and customer satisfaction creates better outcomes, and these provide the basis for the inward circle's link between beliefs, thought, and behavior that collectively revolve around mindsets. In this chapter, we explored how this linkage is the basis for the incredible power of habits. We have seen how people can use habits to accomplish incredible things. As the story of Paul O'Neill and Alcoa shows, keystone habits—like a requirement for a unit president to report an injury and provide a plan for ensuring the injury does not recur—can produce incredible changes that transform entire organizations in far-reaching ways. O'Neill set out to improve safety, and he also improved communication, efficiency, and productivity. Habits can take us to a place where willpower becomes automatic, and we can use the power of rituals to help organize our days and increase morale and even productivity. As we saw in the case of Starbucks, Willpower is like a muscle: it can be strengthened through exercise. Make the cultivation of productive habits a priority, and you will be astonished at the results you and your organization achieve.

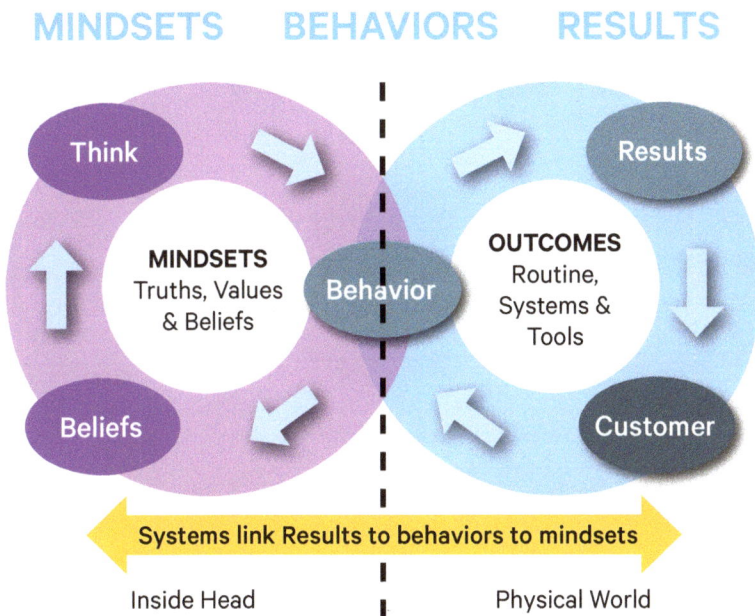

Figure 3.1—Brings the two circles together (©Action New Thinking)

Eventually, the two circles evolved into a double infinity diagram with 'behaviors' at the center, as shown in Figure 3.2 as the 'Mindset Framework that drives results and 'beliefs driving thinking and sustainable results.

> **?** In concluding this chapter, reflect on some of these questions before moving on to the next chapter:
>
> - Have you defined your current set of beliefs around your desired behaviors?
> - What are your team's beliefs around these desired behaviors?
> - Are your team's current experiences reinforcing the desired beliefs?
> - Are your values aligned with these beliefs?
> - Are your corporate values aligned with the desired beliefs, and does your team see the link?

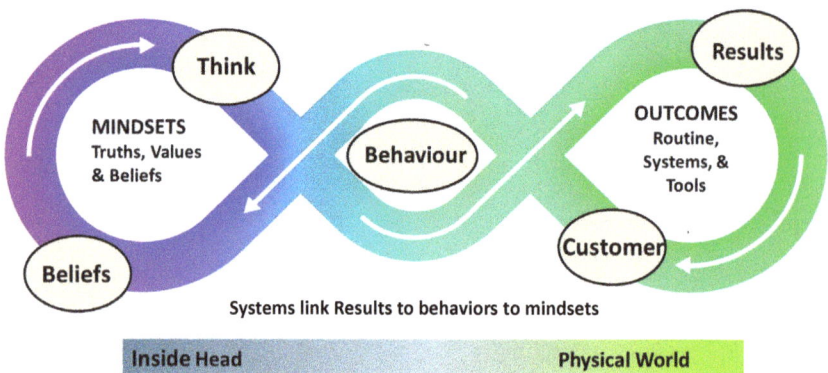

Figure 3.2—Thinking Framework for Enterprise Excellence
(©Action New Thinking)

Character

We should be clear about the importance of character. Character is the first element in establishing a trusting workplace. Warren Buffett often says:

> "In looking for people to hire, you look for three qualities: integrity, intelligence, and energy. And if they don't have the first, the other two will kill you."

This is very good advice. You've probably heard the truism that "Character is doing the right thing when nobody's looking." Think about how important that is for your organization: the ability to trust that people will do what they're supposed to do even when you're not around.

Character and competence are the two key elements to establishing trust. However, it is how we communicate those to others that is critical. Here are two videos that explain this:

1. The Trust Quadrant - Why Character and Competence are Key https://lnkd.in/evBv5u7k
2. Character - the first element explained: https://lnkd.in/gC6BUzk2

Here's a Formula:

(Character + Confidence) x Communication = High Levels of Trust.

Communication isn't just making public speeches and making statements. It is much more than that. The communication I am referring to is about who you are as a person. One of my favorite quotes about character comes from Ralph Waldo Emerson:

> "Who you are thunders so loudly I cannot hear what you are saying."

Character comprises Integrity and Intent.

Integrity is:

- Congruence - Do I do what I say I will do? Am I consistent?
- Humility - What's right vs. I am right. Can I say, "I don't know"?
- Courage - Do I take the easy way? Am I firm in my values? Will I stand up for fairness?
- Intent is:
- Motive - Is this for me or them? Do I assume positive intent?
- Agenda - Is this for mutual benefit? Do I give credit to others?
- Clarity - Do I declare my intent? Am I willing to discuss my intent with others? Do I create confidence in others?

Linking Experiences to Beliefs

At the Shingo Conference 2024 in Orlando, Bullfrog Spas presented a compelling concept about how staff experiences shape their beliefs.

- Their experiences shape their beliefs.
- Their beliefs drive their behaviors.
- The behaviors determine their results.

So, the character of a leader is not just to define the **Behaviors** in the organization but to develop the **Experiences** of the staff to shape their **Beliefs.**

Throughout this book, I have driven the importance of the beliefs to drive sustainable behaviors.

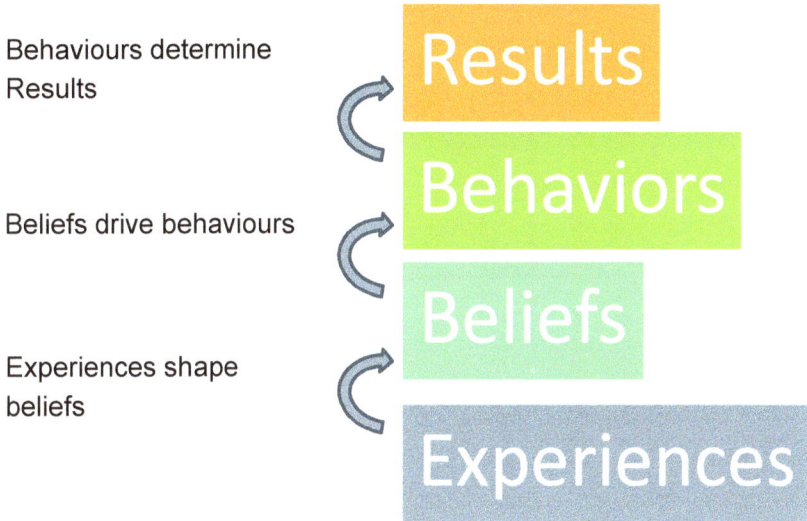

Behaviours determine
Results

Beliefs drive behaviours

Experiences shape
beliefs

Figure 3.2—Experiences link to beliefs (©Action New Thinking)

While the common adage, "The customer is always right," is important, Sir Richard also follows his own beliefs. He is quoted as saying:

> "Clients do not come first. Employees come first. If you take care of your employees, they will take care of the clients."

Sir Richard believes that his philosophy, "Employees come first," is the reason behind his success. He respects his staff, taking the time to meet them in person and listen to them. To prove he is serious about this business ethic, he has put himself in their shoes and gained a genuine insight into their working conditions. This has made employees loyal to their boss and proud to work for Virgin. Sir Richard also believes in having fun and is well-known for his charisma and eccentric behavior. One of the most famous examples of this was when Branson served as an air hostess on an international flight!

On quizzing why staff experience was essential, he explained that staff experience reinforced the thinking that drove the behaviors of staff to deliver exceptional customer experience every time. When pushed, Sir Richard agreed that the thinking was the unconscious thinking he was talking about, and the experience is something to have to maintain every day to reinforce their beliefs on delivering customer experience.

Figure 3.3 shows how all these concepts align with Professor Edgar Shein's Organizational Culture Model.

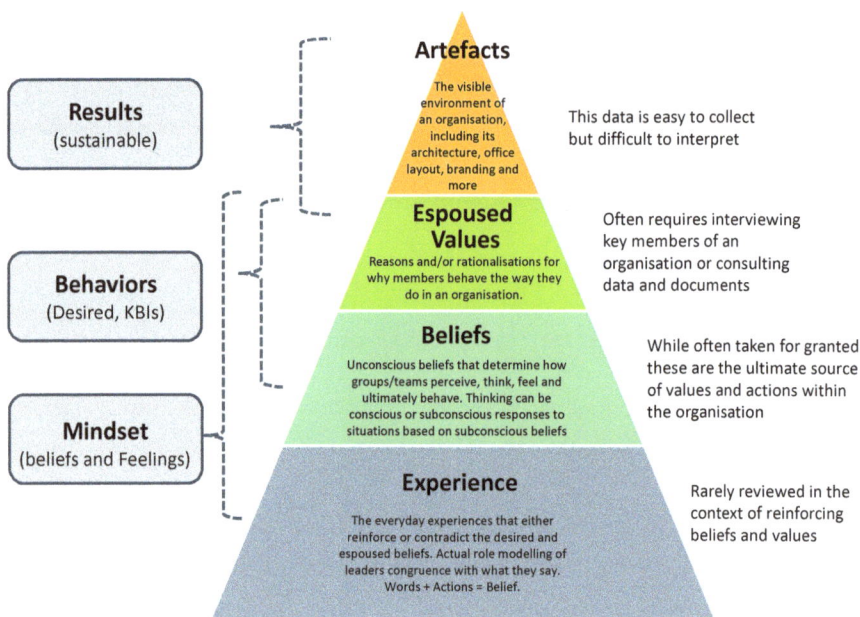

Figure 3.3—Alignment with Edgar Schein Organizational Culture Model (©Action New Thinking)

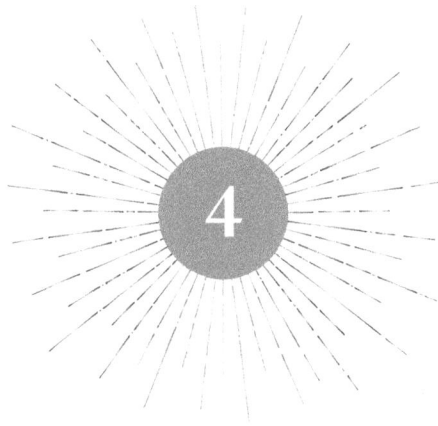

Updating the 4+2 Operating System

In the previous chapters, I have developed a mindset framework for Enterprise Excellence that brings to the forefront the underlying beliefs required to enable the desired behaviors in life and deliver continuously improving and sustainable business results.

Soon after joining the Commonwealth Bank of Australia (CBA) as the head of Productivity, I sat in a coffee shop pondering how it all fitted together in my head so I could inspire everyone in the organization to use the 2 systems of culture and capability build. CBA had a model of 3Cs (see book 4+1 by Jones et al. for more details) being Capability, Culture and Capacity:

- Capability was around delivering strong expertise to solve complex problems through Lean Six Sigma Green, Black and Master Black Belts.

- The culture was around unifying teams to solve problems within their control.

- Capacity was around delivering business results (savings and customer experience improvements) to continue to justify the investment in culture and capability.

I took three napkins to draw a picture of the operating model that was the heart of the Productivity program (page 42 in 4+1 2nd edition). That was over 10 years ago, and I have updated the Operating System to now be 4+2 because of experience where organizations are challenged to get strategy alignment down to front-line workers. Another key to this update has been the development of the underlying beliefs of each of the six habits so they can become subconscious thinking, i.e., habits. Figure 4.1 shows the updated 4+2 Operating System.

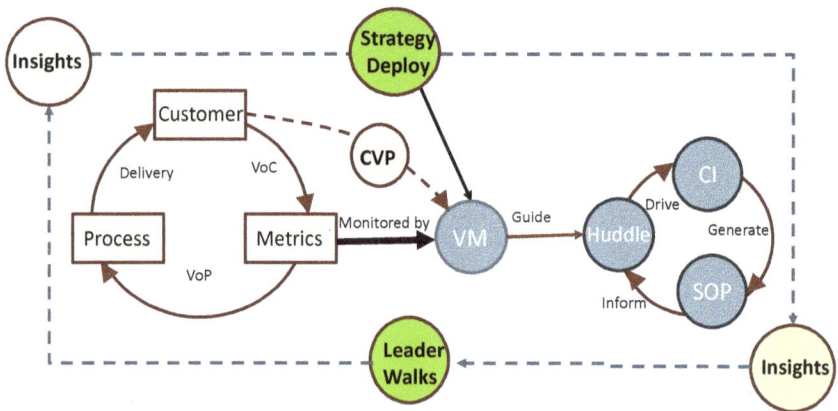

Figure 4.1—Updated 4+2 Operating System (©Action New Thinking)

The key visual difference was changing a square for strategy to becoming a leadership habit of 'Strategy Deployment,' changing SOP to Standard Work and changing the name of Gemba to Lean Leader Walks, as the Japanese word Gemba can be polarizing. The important revelation and missing piece of the puzzle tying all the strategic thinking (to metrics, how to evolve) and all the linkages to standard work (VM & Huddles), CVP so that front-line people understand how their daily work aligns and contribute to the metrics and delivering the business strategy.

Let's explore each of the six habits working as a system and their underlying beliefs.

Visual Management Habit [1]

The Visual Management habit is both a habit and a tool. The Visual Management Board (VMB) serves as a focal point for teams to review performance, set priorities, solve problems, and manage continuous improvement activities. The purpose of this habit, and the use of the boards, is to create transparency—and the boards are tools toward that end. Fortunately, VMB is easy to install—but the bad news is that many teams struggle with them. Fortunately, the main pitfalls and problems teams encounter with VMBs and the visual management habit—that is to say, using the VMB—are easy to summarize, and with a little persistence and effort, they can be overcome.

An important issue that occurs again and again with VMBs might be described as the "wallpaper problem." This happens when a company installs a VMB, and it is duly covered with masses of lovely graphs, each painstakingly created for a team purpose... and then no one pays attention to it. A VMB, in this scenario, is essentially a prop, a novelty item—but not a useful tool and not the basis for a good visual management habit.

Another issue that can crop up is the use of the VMB as a one-way communication board. It becomes a bulletin, created to benefit the boss and the occasional visitor—but not an interactive tool and not one that produces many actual initiatives. This issue is best understood as a breakdown or failure of the intended dialogue that the VMB is supposed to stimulate.

Similarly, the VMB can become the "boss' board," something the team creates to benefit the boss so the boss can track what's happening. Here, the boss derives some actual benefit from the board, but the problem is that it creates more work for the team and delivers little in the way of actual value for them. In some of these cases, the problem occurs because the boss creates the board for the team, and this means no one understands it. There is no sense among the team that the board is relevant, and so they do not see value in it, and there is little engagement.

Finally, sometimes, VMBs are treated as single tools and not linked to others. The problem with this is that they are not integrated into the management process. Fortunately, these problems are solved. The overall goal is to have the VMB serve as an essential element of the system of improvement—to have it be a habit that drives and supports all other habits in the organization. The team must find it useful and own its presence in the organization.

An important facilitation strategy here is to have each team develop its visual management board. While this may create challenges for leaders to accept, it is very much in keeping with an essential part of team engagement—namely, for the leaders to accept that they need to let go and give their teams autonomy to do things such as develop their VMBs. And teams can be equipped to do this if they are given the proper understanding and if the board is allowed to evolve through regular cycles of Plan, Do, Check, and Act (PDCA).

The key point to realize is that the real habit is not the board itself—the board is merely a tool—but making things transparent, and this is done by updating the visual boards. What the pitfalls above have in common is that they are, at some level, mistaking the trees for the forest: they lack an appreciation of the big picture and treat the board as something much less than it is intended to be. It is one of many places you will embark on your improvement journey.

With this in view, the **purpose** of the habit becomes clear: to figure out which conversations the team wants to have in a group huddle environment. These conversations should be guided by certain underlying beliefs, particularly an understanding of value in the eyes of customers. This means that the board should be regularly updated with fresh data and metrics, including customer value propositions. The process is further refined by leaders, who ensure the right Key Performance Indicators (KPIs) and Key Behavioral Indicators (KBIs). The KBIs are indicators, whether activities, actions, or tasks, that drive change to the KPIs, which are leading indicators.

We've highlighted the importance of beliefs repeatedly in this book, so let's underscore the relevance of belief in this context. The pitfalls associated with the VMB can all be addressed by helping your employees develop the right beliefs about the VMB. When they stop seeing it as the "boss's board" or a one-way communication board and see it as an important habit for figuring out in advance what conversations they want to have in their group huddles, they will believe that it can save them time and provide a helpful organizational and communication tool—and this will help with the deeper entrenchment of the habit.

Properly implemented, this habit will synchronize beautifully with others, particularly regarding the conversations teams have in their huddles. These conversations will identify opportunities for them to start the Go, Observe habit and provide a link to continuous improvement. They will also drive quality performance conversations in huddles. This habit is very much a cornerstone of the whole program.

Once you understand that the entire purpose of this habit is to foster transparency, many things become much clearer and easier. If you want to test the effectiveness of your organization's visual management habit, first ask people if they know what the key goals are for the business over the next couple of years. This question checks for alignment: Are they aligned with the overall strategy and plan?

Second, I will ask them what they will do differently to help meet those goals. This question checks for engagement: Are they prepared to go the distance to help put the plan into practice? With alignment and engagement, the visual management habit should be effective at establishing and cultivating transparency in your workplace and providing a means of assessing performance.

Huddles Habit [2]

Above, we covered the VMB and the associated visual management habits, and we broached the subject of huddles. The connection here is that any VMB is only as good as the quality of the conversations it provokes within the workplace. Huddles should be systematized, with planned meeting times and durations, and they should be scheduled in a sequence such that leaders can be present at more than one meeting on a given day.

A good rule of thumb during a huddle is about 10-15 minutes, and there should be careful coaching of the teams regarding simple operating rules to help make the whole thing more efficient. For example, the one-minute rule is that if a topic relates to, say, just two people rather than the whole team, they have one minute to discuss it. This helps keep things on track and moving along. Some teams like to have a clock with 15 minutes marked in red, and some even decide to impose penalties for people who are not prepared or who turn up late. Let your teams experiment and do what is best for them, so long as the focus remains action-oriented and teams get value from the discussion.

Overall, a good huddle will have a few identified features, starting with being short and focused. It is important to respect everyone's time. Second, a huddle should review recent performance against targets to assess how well a team is doing. Third, huddles need to celebrate success: team members need to feel the freedom to celebrate their hard work. Fourth, huddles should establish agreement on priorities. There should also be agreement on actions to be taken, including who is to undertake them and on/by what date(s).

It's also important for huddles to be facilitated by different members of the team since this helps to reduce dominance by one or more charismatic personalities and promotes engagement overall. And again, huddles should take place at a fixed time and day so everyone knows when to expect them. Finally, they should also be sequenced according to the operating rhythm of the team for overall performance and effectiveness.

- What does participation in a good huddle look like?
- For associates/employees, it generally means contributing proactively to the huddle discussion.

- For managers, it means regularly attending huddles to listen, learn, and support the team.
- For leaders, it is a chance to show that the huddles are important by visiting them and asking about them.

One crucially important test that one should be certain to run to check if the huddles are effective is to see if the teams are now spending less time on meetings than they were before the introduction of both the visual management habit and VMB, as well as huddles. Review the current list of meetings and get rid of most of them. Ask yourself and others why this, that, or the other meeting subject is not covered in a huddle.

Over time, huddles can be improved as teams learn to maximize their potential for communication, action, and accountability, in keeping with their purpose of identifying opportunities for continuous improvement and Gemba. If associates and front-line employees regularly update the VMB with information, it should be simple to use the huddle to share how the team is delivering. Also, managers can use the huddles to clarify expectations around purpose and mission.

A shared set of underlying beliefs should also guide huddles, particularly the idea that everyone on the team should know how well things are or are not going, i.e., whether the team is winning or losing. Team members also need to believe that they are better at identifying improvements together than they would be if they tried to do so separately as individuals.

In addition to a shared set of underlying beliefs about how well or poorly things are going, huddles need to be animated by a shared set of beliefs about why the team should do them. Do people believe in using huddles as short, focused sessions for improving communication, action, and accountability? Do they believe huddles are better if everyone participates? Over time, seek to cultivate these beliefs in your employees as they work at the huddles.

With all of this in view, teams can engage in huddles in keeping with ideal behaviors, including short, focused performance reviews, ideally a maximum of 15 minutes. They can also discuss gaps in performance and collaborate to make informed decisions. The KBIs they should focus on include respectfully challenging the group and guiding itself rather than being guided by the company standards.

One other thing to remember is that, particularly in the early stages, the key to good huddles is ensuring that everyone has a sense that the environment is safe. Leaders can help to foster a sense of safety by role-playing the huddle, making sure everyone is on board with the basic purpose and will follow a systematic sequence in discussing the visual board. The coach might start by asking what the purpose of the huddle is, and the leader might say, "We want to have the right conversations." From there, the coach can draw the leader out, all the while helping people to understand the underlying mentality and purpose of the huddle.

Over time, teams will become better and more accomplished at engaging in huddles and will have less and less of a problem advancing them. All the same, still be engaged with how everyone is feeling and ask about achievements and blockers. Above all, keep the conversation moving and engaged to make sure the huddle does not begin to feel like a meeting. The purpose of the huddle is to replace conventional meetings for the most part.

Continuous Improvement Habit [3]

Now that we've covered Visual Management and the Huddles, we're positioned to discuss the third habit, Continuous Improvement, the heart of the improvement engine. The basic idea is simple: every day, we should strive to improve the customer experience while making the process of doing so simpler for ourselves and our colleagues. This habit uses common structured problem-solving to fix problems at their root causes and to test solutions to see if they are good for the problems at hand.

This habit is driven by underlying beliefs in improvement and the idea of improvement as a part of who we, the organization, are. Improvement is not simply a thing we do sometimes; it is a thing we all do all the time, every day and everywhere in the organization because we are seeking perfection. This means that to get the most out of this habit, your employees need to believe in the importance of ongoing improvement. They need to believe that improvement is possible and desirable: that it can help us to do better for the customer and to solve problems for ourselves and our teammates.

This habit connects with, and should generally be integrated with and informed by, the two previous ones: huddles should help to identify opportunities and set priorities for continuous improvement, with the visual management board fostering transparency.

Additionally, VMB serves another important role regarding continuous improvement: making sure that there is tight alignment with business priorities aligned to strategy. The key pitfall regarding this habit is that all too often, CI activities are driven by the things that people feel are important—which may or may not actually be the things that will drive a better customer experience more efficiently. Integrating this habit into

VMB is powerful precisely because it lets teams see that their improvement activities are valued and have a positive impact on all concerned.

Simple frameworks, such as the Plan, Do, Check, Act (PDCA) cycle, are vital for properly implementing CI to encourage widespread adoption at all levels. The PDCA cycle is important for keeping things simple and making it relatively quick and easy to implement a CI idea while making sure everyone is following a standard structure. However, here is a word of caution: all too often, organizations try to force-fit PDCA or the Define, Measure, Analyze, Improve and Control (DMAIC) to everything when it is important to make sure each is used and to make certain everyone understands they are to be applied to different activities. For example, PDCA is excellent for CI activities, but DMAIC is better for significant projects, typically those supported by certified Lean Six Sigma green and black belts. PDCA is better for continuous improvement and bottom-up projects, while DMAIC is better for discontinuous improvement or top-down projects.

In developing the CI habit, it is important to make sure everyone understands the reward and recognition system for the implementation of improvements. These rewards and recognitions should be in place at the team, department, division, and whole business levels. People respond better to a great deal of low-level, frequent recognition, as opposed to sporadic recognition from a massive bureaucratic process, even if the recognition sporadically doled out is excellent. The improvements should also be tracked with effective but simple cost-benefit analyses so that there is a clear understanding of value-driven benefits, societal benefits, and performance-driven benefits for all staff members of an organization.

For associates, this may look like a willingness and ability to identify continuous improvement opportunities that do two things regularly:

1) improve the customer experience and 2) make the process more efficient. The role of managers is important, too, since they need to coach and encourage the application of PDCA and structured problem-solving, especially by asking questions about the process of problem-solving that people use to arrive at a solution. For leaders, the key responsibility is to make sure the system for managing continuous improvement ideas implementation is simple and enables fast and frequent feedback and recognition.

Ideally, this habit will lead to teams identifying improvement everywhere, every day. Teams will collaborate across the organization to make sure improvement is not siloed but shared by everyone. Teams should focus on understanding gaps to achieve their aspirations, and they should develop, maintain, and improve systems of work to ensure continuous improvement. This is something that one can track with the KBIs of coached problem-solving and leading improvement initiatives at the required level of the organization.

When this habit is properly implemented, there should be a strong sense of improvement driven by the identified gaps on the VMB, strongly focusing on improving results, linked strategy, and alignment to purpose; you will see and have an improvement culture because the improvement engine has momentum. Building the skills of everyone involved needs to be a strong focus on creating a mindset of continuous improvement. Also, improvement should be measured and defined based on systems of work, procedures, processes, and standards.

A carefully cultivated habit of continuous improvement synchronizes with the two previous habits and elevates an organization to new heights. Every day becomes a quest for greater perfection, for delivering better value and results for the customer while simplifying as much as possible.

You're likely to find that morale rises as people see their hard work paying off and achieve things they never thought were possible. Coach your people, implement a PDCA cycle, and watch continuous improvement transform your organization.

Standard Work Habit [4]

We've now seen important building blocks for creating change and improvement within an organization. One thing that they all have in common is a general sense of standardization. In keeping with this theme, the fourth habit is the Standard Work habit or standard operating procedures. Standard operating procedures provide a baseline standard from which improvement can be measured and implemented, and, if properly designed, will help with and accelerate process performance rather than becoming onerous complications.

What is the purpose of standard operating procedures? The answer is simple: they are designed to verify improvements that move metrics. This is fundamental to why they are so important and connects with the underlying beliefs that drive standard operating procedures: If our organization works as intended, following a set system of processes, standards, procedures, and work systems will enable the organization to deliver on its strategy and provide value for the customer.

However, here, we should pause and recognize that standard work has a bad rap. Too often, they are viewed as necessary evils, tools for ensuring compliance. This is because they are overly complicated, difficult to locate, and out of date. This discredits them and leads to frustration: people try to get around them rather than viewing them as useful tools.

Getting around these stumbling blocks is important, and it can be done with a simple attitude adjustment—and, if necessary, a redesign of standard work. Properly implemented and understood, standard work is excellent because it is a useful "single source of truth," a paradigm by which compliance and performance can be measured helpfully.

To ensure your employees have good experiences with standard work, begin by keeping them simple. People don't want needless complexity, so keep it simple and intuitive. You need to make sure you involve the people who will perform the procedure in the design phase: this increases a sense of ownership and morale and helps them to feel listened to. Once implemented, the standard operating procedure should have visual aids, such as pictures, screenshots, and simple flowcharts.

Once a standard work is implemented, it should be an integral part of the improvement process. New hires should be trained in it, and they should be taught to internalize its reasons. It is useful to develop a few simple questions that can help people understand the power of standard work, such as "How do you know what the best way is to execute this process?" and "What is the standard for this process?" And if someone wants to make improvements—and even if they do not—ask them, "How do you know if suggested changes will improve the current process?"

The standard work should ideally become gospel because it is useful to have a standard for truth. In this vein, it is critical to make sure there is a simple process and clear ownership for managing and updating standard operating procedures—which, like everything, need to be managed and updated. They also need to be easy to find and easy to keep up to date. They need to be integrated into the continuous improvement cycle so that everyone understands the need to update them to reflect changes introduced by other improvements. If an improvement is made, it will require changes to standard operating procedures.

Over time, your employees should develop beliefs about the importance of standard work. They should see that having clear and universally understood standards for how to do things is safer, more efficient, and generally better for everyone—the employees, management, and consumers. When they believe that standard work is better and more efficient, they'll be more enthusiastic about it.

As standard work is implemented across an organization, you should see more progress toward ideal behaviors, namely for teams to follow standard work processes and procedures. Teams should also be expected to conduct verification activities to measure impact and to identify opportunities for improvement. KBIs include actions raised from verification activities and a sense that employees and teams recognize ideal behaviors seen during verification activities.

Properly implemented, standard work will verify results by documenting process and procedure improvements, connecting them with the continuous improvement habit. Ideally, the result will be a positive feedback loop, a virtuous cycle in which standard work will become the basis for future improvement. There should also be a shared sense that systems underpin the organization's strategy and the work that the organization does.

As standard work transforms your organization, you're likely to see positive changes on all fronts. Associates who may have once shunned the whole idea of standard operating procedures will make regular use of them, contribute to their creation, and help to keep them up to date as improvements are made. Managers will make sure people are trained to use them, and they will also ensure that people understand why they are so important. Finally, leaders will make sure the system to manage standard operating procedures remains simple and easy to use, that it is easily accessible and easily updated, and that such changes are made effectively, followed by communication.

Standard work is often the bugbear of an organization, but as we have now seen, they do not have to be. Try implementing the insights we have discussed here, and watch the changes sweep your organization as your employees learn to take ownership of standard operating procedures.

Leader Walks (Gemba) Habit [+1]

We've covered several habits that can help your organization level up productivity. But how are you, the leader, supposed to know the reality on the ground? Charts and meetings do not always capture realities for front-line workers. Enter our fifth habit, the Leader's Walk or the Gemba walk. The word Gemba comes to us from Japanese, and it means "actual place," as in the actual place where any value-creating work occurs: a shop floor, say, or a workstation, any place where employees create value for the organization. The purpose of doing a Gemba walk—or a leader walk, for our purposes here—is simple and easy to understand. It provides you, the leader, with the ability to see reality and learn from the very place in which your employees are creating value.

With this said, let's clarify what a leader's walk is and what it is not. A leader walk needs to be the best way to understand what's happening in your organization—and that means it cannot be a "royal tour" with lots of handshaking as your employees bow and scrape. Remember, the whole idea is to learn what is actually going on in your organization on the ground: you want to understand, not showboat and be flattered. A leader walk should also be a process for coaching and developing people's skills:

after all, this helps the workforce to improve at what they do, and that is good for them, for the organization, and for the customer. This also means that the leader walk must be about observing and listening rather than "management by walkabout": you are not there to micro-manage but to listen, learn, and help them. Observing and listening are the ideal behaviors for a leader walk, with giving feedback and instructions occupying a much smaller role: go into a leader walk with a will and desire to learn.

What this means is that a leader walk is a good opportunity for firsthand engagement and a cultural health check. This means it cannot be an opportunity to catch people and call them out for doing the wrong thing. We want to help our employees become better so the organization can do more of what it does for the customer and do it better. Think of it as a chance to check the True North cascade and understand the same: how do people see the overall goal, the polestar toward which everyone should be working in the organization? With this in view, you can see how the leader's walk cannot be guided by a pre-prepared script with a set list of questions: you need to be open to what you might see and learn and able and willing to address any issues you might become aware of.

With that said, there are a few questions you can and should ask yourself before embarking on a leader walk. These questions will help you to approach it constructively and get the most out of it. Ask yourself what defines value for your customers, where that value is created, and who the people create that value. Finally, ask how you can best serve them so they can serve the customer.

Leader walks are best learned by practicing. Think of them as a key part of the Check in the Plan, Do, Check, Act (PDCA) cycle because that is exactly what they are: a chance to check on what everyone is doing and how well they are doing it, and how you, the leader, can help them do it better. An effective leader walk should leave not only you but also management and associates feeling valued. Associates and managers should feel respected because of the leader's walk, and they should feel a greater sense of ownership and pride in the work that they do. For leaders, the leader's walk should give a better understanding of the process and any issues and should lead to much stronger working relationships. Think of it as a chance to serve, coach, and give recognition.

KBIs for a leader walk concern communication. Have you, the leader, communicated what you have learned from the leader's walk? Have you recognized the ideal behaviors you observed your employees engaging in and praised them for what they have been doing right? Getting this right is important for linking the leader's walk to other habits: do it well, and you can gain valuable insights to inform problem-solving and continuous improvement.

Over time, associates should learn to make sure that their workplace is always leader walk ready, meaning they do not have to make any special preparations for a leader walk. Managers should be able to show that every conversation, and not just formal coaching sessions, provides an opportunity to develop people. Leaders should recognize that every conversation is a chance to listen and learn.

What beliefs will enhance the value of leader walks? The answer is simple: you need to believe in them as an effective tool for enhancing communication and understanding. Your employees need to believe in them as a chance to be seen and heard and to help you understand the realities they are dealing with every day. When everyone sees leader walks as a chance for communication, empathy, and understanding, they will begin to reach their full potential within your organization.

As you gain skills in leader walks, your awareness and ability to use them will mature over time. You're likely to find that, at first, you recognize they are important and have clear expectations for all leaders in your organization to do them. As your awareness matures, you'll see that leader walks are integral to systems of improvement. And with time, as you continue to practice leader walks, you may wish to regularly review them for effectiveness and hone your skills in sharing "lessons learned" with other leaders.

Leader walks are a wonderful and very important tool for optimizing and improving productivity by connecting leaders with the realities on the ground. Over time, you and other leaders in your organization are likely to find that they are indispensable for keeping channels of communication open between leaders, management, and associates and for helping with improvement and creating value. Use the lessons we've discussed here to help you and focus on listening and learning from your employees to foster an understanding of the mentor relationship and commitment to improvement.

Strategy Deployment Habit [+2]

Having covered five productivity habits, we are ready to wrap up this discussion with a look at the sixth habit. This habit ties them all together: the Strategy Deployment habit. This habit is fundamental to achieving and maintaining growth, something many companies struggle with. The solution is to practice strategy planning, establish a roadmap of where one wants to go, and then use strategy deployment to get there. Strategy planning is the map, and strategy deployment is the tactical approach for actually getting there.

To practice strategy deployment, one must define one's targets and connect improvement focus to the factors, systems, processes, and people needed to deliver results. This habit provides clarity on the improvement engine we use to deliver on business strategy, vision, and overall purpose, so we can start with the idea that serving our customers is a key driving core principle. Once we understand customer focus, cascading vision, metrics, and targets, we will be ready to pursue operating perfection based on the underlying beliefs in discipline and the use of strategy to build on our purpose to serve customers, deepening our improvement capabilities and finding ways to eliminate waste. And, too, we will appreciate the need to empower our people, using rhythms and routines to ensure our sustainability.

With this said, there are common pitfalls that many companies run into when trying to cultivate a strategy deployment habit. One notable pitfall is a lack of commitment and involvement from management, and it is easy to see why: when leadership cannot even be bothered to invest in a strategic plan, employees will respond. Strategies also need clear, realistic goals, and an absence of an objective view of the market and significant perspective is another pitfall that trips up many efforts to implement strategies.

Strategies also need to be workable, and that means deploying them cannot be more complex than people can really handle, given the resources available. Excessive complexity is a pitfall that can doom a strategic deployment plan by making it too difficult to understand and implement. Another thing strategy deployments need is a schedule, and so a failure to schedule—or a failure to follow a schedule—represents another pitfall. Reducing strategy to budgeting is another pitfall: you need understanding and commitment; strategy cannot be possible if it is reduced to financial investment. Underestimating required resources is another issue: it is essential to understand what resources a strategy will actually need if it is to be deployed correctly.

A failure to monitor progress is another pitfall. For several reasons, people and groups may deviate from a strategy and strategic objectives. If this goes unchecked for too long, corrective actions may come too late to salvage a strategy. One final common pitfall is the failure to define success in quantifiable terms. Clarity, both as clear goals and clear indicators, is everyone's friend: the clearer the goals and indicators, the better. This is important for making adjustments as necessary.

When deploying strategy, leaders should show **ideal behaviors** in the form of linking mission, vision, purpose, behavior, systems, and strategy deployment to business outcomes. At the strategy review stage, data collection and preparation are key: one needs to understand the organization's capabilities and financials and the market realities it is trying to respond to and engage with. Reflection on performance, using data on sales trends, and understanding root causes are important as well. Analyzing strategic opportunities is also important.

In the second step, Hoshin Deployment, the focus should be on the Strategic Value Stream Analysis (VSA) Deep Dives and building a top-level Hoshin Matrix Design with breakthrough goals and priorities for improvement, as well as targets to be achieved and accountable individuals. This is connected to the Hoshin Kanri lean strategy. Hoshin Kanri refers to the "compass" or "true north" and connotes setting a guiding direction for a company. The key insight is that if you want everyone pointed toward the true north, everyone needs to understand it and *commit*. At this stage, the strategy is cascaded down to different levels of the organization, and everyone gets ready to work on breakthrough priorities.

The third stage, breakthrough priorities, entails quantifying and monitoring the improvement priorities previously set. Each improvement priority and its targets should be listed on a chart, and objectives should be quantified for each month. The mission control room should be set up, and Hoshin meetings should be held to monitor the progress of the strategy implementation. Improvements should be deployed with as much rapidity and efficacy as possible.

Finally, in the Hoshin Review stage, regular reviews should correct deviations and improve the process. This includes monthly Hoshin reviews and countermeasures to correct deviations from partial goals. Another key aspect of this stage is the Hoshin retrospective, which reflects on the process, identifies improvement opportunities, and makes decisions for the next cycle. There is also a need to do a forward-looking strategic review on a quarterly and 6-monthly process routine to ensure you are indeed working on the right priorities as a team/organization. This process is important for ensuring effective implementation of strategy and encouraging continuous improvement and alignment throughout the organization. Work at strategy deployment, and your organization will lock in and accelerate productivity gains.

Strategy deployment works best when people genuinely believe in it, and that means seeing the results. Involve your employees in every stage of the process as you design and deploy strategies: not only will they help you design better strategies and produce better deployments, but they will also be more likely to believe in the whole process if they understand everything happening and the reasons for it.

Summary

This chapter has summarized how the original 4+1 operating model (Jones, M L et al.) has been updated to '4+2' with the addition of a 6th habit, more information around desired behaviors, KBIs and most importantly, the underlying beliefs of each habit, to make them sustainable interlinked habits. The following table summarizes the key points.

	Habit 1 – Visual Management (VM)	Habit 2 – Huddles	Habit 3- Continuous Improvement (CI)	Habit 4 – Standard Work (SW)	Habit +1 Lean Leader Walks (Gemba)	Habit +2 Strategy Deployment (SD)
High-Level Definition	Habit of continually updating performance data	Short, sharp performance dialogue addressing gaps and trends	Enabling teams to fix problems at root cause within the realm of control.	Lock in new improvements and confirm improvements materialized and moving metrics on VMB.	Leaders were going to see where the work was done and coach teams to solve the problem where the work was done.	Strategy is broken down by level so that each level of the organization can align the daily work to deliver on strategic measures.
Purpose/ Aim/Intent	Enabling what conversations does the team want to have in the huddle?	Identify opportunities for continuous improvement and Gemba	Use common structured problem solving to fix problems at root cause and test solutions.	Verify improvements moving metrics. Lock in solutions into BAU	Need to see reality. Learn from where the work is done.	Provide clarity of improvement engine to deliver on business strategy, vision, and purpose.
Underlying Beliefs	We understand what value in the eyes of our customers is, so they trust us. It is respectful to have up-to-date data to enable the team to make the best decisions. We use the 1–3–10 rule to drive data transparency and inform the Go and See.	Everyone on the team should know how well things are going, i.e., winning or losing. The team is better at identifying improvements than one individual through Gemba.	Improvement is part of who we are. It is done by everyone every day and everywhere in the organization. Working on the right improvements is pivotal to delivering our strategy. We constantly seek perfection and challenge our aspirational targets. We work collaboratively with all stakeholders to deliver value.	Working as intended and following our processes, standards, procedures, and systems of work will enable us to deliver our strategy and value to the customer.	We need to see reality and learn from where the work is done and from those performing the work. We share and communicate the lessons obtained from the Gemba to create value for our people and the customer.	We are disciplined in ensuring we maintain our SD and DM routines because long-term SD and DM built on our purpose, behaviors, and systems are pivotal to our success. We serve our customers through our actions.

Table 4.1—Habits Belief Table (©Action New Thinking)

98

Believe

	Habit 1 – Visual Management (VM)	Habit 2 - Huddles	Habit 3- Continuous Improvement (CI)	Habit 4 – Standard Work (SW)	Habit +1 Lean Leader Walks (Gemba)	Habit +2 Strategy Deployment (SD)
Ideal Behaviors	Regularly update data and metrics, including customer value proposition and VoC. All team members regularly update data and metrics, including customer value proposition and VOC. Leaders ensure the right KPIs are in place to drive transparency and improvement dialogue. All team members ensure appropriate actions are in place and up to date to close the gaps.	The team has short, focused performance reviews, ideally a 15-minute standing. Discussing Gaps, i.e., red and green trends. Teams have short, focused performance discussions, ideally 15 minutes, standing. Discussing the gaps, i.e., reds and green trends. Teams collaborate as a diverse group to make informed decisions.	Teams identify improvement everywhere, every day. Teams collaborate across the organization to ensure improvement is not done in silos. Teams focus on the green as much as the red, seeking to understand the gaps in aspiration. Teams develop, maintain, and improve systems of work to ensure continuous improvement.	Teams follow standard work processes and procedures. Teams conduct verification activities to measure impact and identify improvement opportunities.	We go to the Gemba, with "Big Eyes, Big Ears and Small Mouth." We go to the Gemba to understand the problem and understand or obtain the solution from those who do the work. We recognized ideal behaviors at the Gemba and addressed non-ideal behaviors.	Leaders link vision, mission, purpose, behaviors, systems, and strategy deployment to business outcomes. Leaders and team members embrace VOC thinking. Leaders ensure that conversations on both horizontal and vertical value streams are taking place.
Linkage to other habits	What conversations must the team have in their huddles? Identifies the opportunities for the team to start the Go and See. Provides the link to continuous improvement. Drive quality performance conversations at huddles.	Identify areas to solve problems and go to Gemba. Drives conversation from the VMB from identified opportunities for continuous improvement and going to the Gemba.	Conducting improvement from identified gaps on the VMB and improved results linked to strategy and aligned to purpose. Building the skills of our people creates a continuous improvement mindset. Measure and define improvement based on systems of work, procedures, processes, and standards.	Verify results documenting process/ procedure improvements. Standard work becomes the basis for future improvement. Systems underpin our strategy and the work we do.	Process to inform problem-solving and continuous improvement. Broaden understanding of potential gaps in actual work performed and alignment to work as intended.	Providing the 'why' behind the metrics on the VMB. Ensuring we are working on the right improvement at the right time. We should show the customer that we care about their value. Align all mindsets on performance and confirm KPIs and KBI golden threat.

99

Think of the 4+2 Operating System as a recipe for change: it provides habits that can help you jumpstart implementing the insights of the outward and inward wheels and create a culture of continuous improvement in your organization. The Visual Management habit, if implemented correctly, should serve as a useful way to promote accountability and transparency and to drive change through the group huddles. Once everyone understands what they will discuss in the group huddles, the huddles should be a productive forum for ensuring change toward productive goals identified for continuous improvement. This takes us to the continuous improvement habit, which is focused on customer service focused on ensuring the customer has the best experience. As we have seen, the Plan, Do, Check, Act (PDCA) cycle is important for properly implementing this habit. This connects with the fourth habit, that of creating standard operating procedures or a standard work habit. If there is a clear baseline standard, improvement can be measured and implemented with reference to it—and an improvement is defined in terms of moving metrics. With this in view, the leader walks or "Gemba" habit is important to make sure leaders understand daily operations and can help employees and learn from them. This connects with the strategy deployment habit: planning a strategy to provide a map, defining one's targets, and connecting the improvement focus to those factors needed to deliver results.

Figure 4.2 shows how the 4+2 habits link to the PDCA cycle and the core questions for each habit.

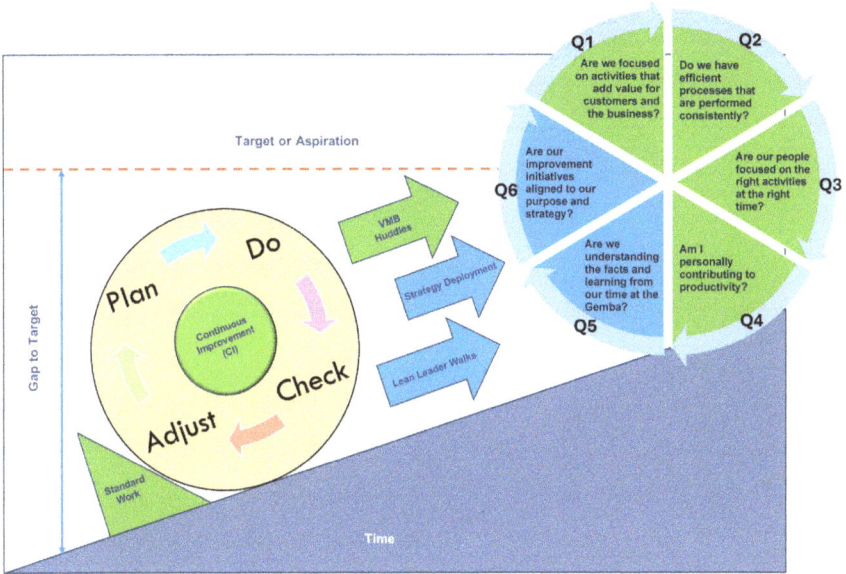

Figure 4.2—PDCA link to 4+2 habits
(© Action New Thinking & Odyssey Alliance)

(?) In concluding this chapter, reflect on some of these questions before moving on to the next chapter:

- What operating systems do we have?
- Do the components link to enable each other?
- Is my system and tools driving my desired behavior?

5

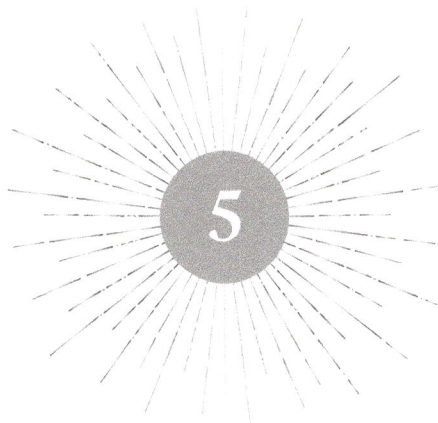

Coaching Framework

In coaching, the role of the coach is to help the pupil understand not only what is true but also to explore others' perspectives.

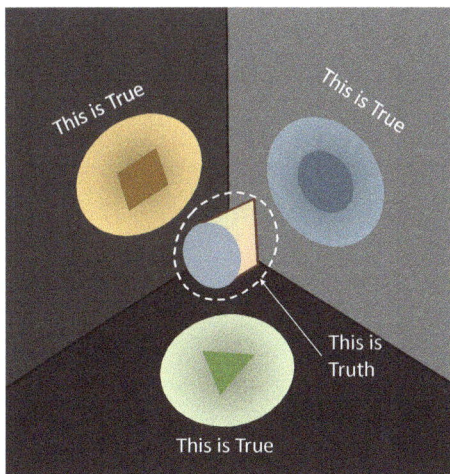

Figure 5.0—Perspectives of true and truth (©Action New Thinking)

What is the importance of gathering feedback at all levels of the delivery system? Perspectives on what is "true" are relative to the points of view at each level of the organization. The "truth" is an amalgamation of all those perspectives viewed objectively.

> *"In order to understand ourselves, others, and the world around us, we need to be able to change and adapt our perspectives."*
> —Albert Einstein

Introduction to Coaching

Leaders need to use human nature to help to accomplish their visions. A coaching strategy lets the leader create gentle ripples to influence others to embrace change rather than resist it through a directive style. Coaching also lets the project leader grow through developing their thinking rather than because the sponsor gives them the answer.

Most organizations and sponsors talk about coaching their team, but as soon as the project is on the critical path, the sponsor shirks away from a coaching role, straight past mentor and into a directive role. Sometimes, coaching is seen merely as a passive skill, only applied when the project manager comes to the sponsor with a problem. I have learned that this is easily rectified when the sponsor does not abdicate responsibility for the project by delegating it to a project manager.

> (?) I have found that as soon as I introduce the leader to the chef/restaurant analogy and tell them that their reputation is still on the line, they realize the need to guide the project leader by asking a few pertinent questions. When I see a leader shift to the directing mode, I usually ask only one or maybe two questions – how does the project leader feel when you dictate to them what to do, and how empowered do they feel, or how can you as their sponsor help them learn for themselves from this situation?

Coaching does not mean imposing one's vision but facilitating opportunities for team members to accept and embrace your vision as a project sponsor. Because of coaching, the team will be focused on the goal and perform at their best through their initiative.

There are several coaching models that a Project Sponsor could adopt. What they all have in common is that they are conviction-driven, dynamic, and participative. Coaching must also be honest, truthful, and understanding of people's needs and motivations. The focus must be on action and the development of new ideas.

Beliefs matter a great deal in the realm of coaching. What you and the people you are trying to help believe about coaching and the relationship will affect how effective you both are and whether or not you get out of it, which you are hoping. Believe that you, as the coach, can help and encourage your team members, and you will be better equipped to understand them and connect with them—and with any luck, they'll believe in you as well.

According to Keith Rosen, author of *Coaching Salespeople Into Sales Sponsors*, a coaching edge lets the manager give his people the "tough, edgy support often required to propel people to the next level of success while being mutually supportive and empowering," and without tarnishing their pure intentions, and maintaining the commitment of the workers.

> Here are examples of questions illustrating how the coaching edge may be used:
>
> - Can I point something out to you that may be tough to look at right now?
> - Can I share with you what I see, and then we can work this out together?
> - There's something that I see that may be uncomfortable to hear, and I want to make sure that you are ready to hear it. Is it okay if I move forward in discussing this with you?
> - Do I have permission to say something to you each time I notice you are reverting to your old destructive habits or behaviors?
> - Can I push you a little harder to develop a better way to manage your schedule that will double your productivity each day?

According to Ken Blanchard, renowned management and leadership expert, there are four stages of leadership coaching and participation:

1. Directing – The coach instructs individuals who lack knowledge on new competencies required (e.g., technical, advanced statistical, leadership, team building, and people skills) until the member gains new insights, a sufficient understanding of the job, and a new appreciation of their experiences.

2. Coaching – The team member could already independently perform his functions with minimal assistance. The coach

intervenes only when there is a problem to be resolved, such as when a project goal is not met.

3. Delegating – After sufficient training and coaching, the member masters the required skills, competently performs his functions without help and displays desired behaviors. The coach delegates full responsibility.

4. Supporting – The coach is relegated to a scaffolding role. They continue to drive peak performance through encouragement and recognition of accomplishments.

Practically, this means a Project Sponsor should:

- Make an inventory of knowledge, skills, and talents at the individual and team levels, as well as their needs and motivations.

- Diagnose strengths and weaknesses of the team members; identify opportunities for improvements vis-à-vis project goals and performance standards.

- Identify points of resistance to change; establish reasonable change goals within the project.

- Craft a coaching strategy to enhance influence and coaching effectiveness, which incorporates a recognition and reward system and evaluation criteria.

- Review responsibilities and action steps and confirm commitment from team members.

- Delegate new roles and responsibilities and provide scaffolding to develop competence.

When a sponsor sees that the project team or one of its members is going wayward, they should step in and offer coaching. Coaching is not limited to the development of knowledge and skills to enhance individual and team performance. Coaching is also about guiding the team when their commitment wavers or when their efforts become inconsistent. Through a coaching strategy skillfully used, the sponsor can lead individuals to look at their strengths and capabilities and tap into their energy and talents to solve problems on their own. In this sense, coaching has that unique capability to induce workers to honor their commitment, thus ascribing accountability to themselves.

Coaching may also be used to clarify issues and problems. Sponsors should remember that improvement projects are often most vulnerable after the initial phase when the effects (or the turbulence) of change efforts start to peak. Coaching skills come into play to guide the team to rethink and refocus. However, the sponsor should not go for solving a problem for the team. They should let them discover how to solve it; otherwise, they will become dependent on the sponsor. 4 "C's" of Coaching: Clarity, Criticality, Commitment and Consistency from Sponsor Success (Jones, 2011).

1. Clarity

> *"Effective leaders don't have to be passionate. They don't have to be charming. They don't have to be brilliant... They don't have to be great speakers. What they must be is clear. Above all else, they must never forget the truth that of all the human universals - our need for security, community, clarity, authority, and respect - our need for clarity... is the most likely to engender in our confidence, persistence, resilience, and creativity."*
>
> —Marcus Buckingham
> (The One Thing You Need to Know: About Great Managing,
> Great Leading, and Sustained Individual Success, Free Press, 2005)

If we are not clear about a problem, then we can't fix it. If we do not understand a plan, we can't implement it. When we are uncertain about what we are trying to achieve, we can't get there. Lack of clarity in the parts of a Lean Six Sigma project is antithetical to the principles of Lean Six Sigma because uncertainties and ambiguities waste time and resources.

For the Lean Six Sigma Sponsor, if they are not clear about the benefits of a process improvement project, they cannot sell it to organizational leaders, process owners, or their project team. Real clarity is when the problem or opportunity of the project can be articulated in one to two sentences without using significant inclusion of acronyms, using simple language to avoid ambiguity.

I worked with a sponsor with a PhD and over 25 years of experience in the business. He presented his problem statement as part of the charter. He explained the problem in over 10 minutes, with great detail and many acronyms. While I understood the general principle of his project—his business's employees and contractors had suffered 71 injuries during a year—I was not clear on the urgency.

To help with clarity, I asked the sponsor if his eleven-year-old daughter would have understood his explanation. I stressed the simple rule: unravel the **Complex**, make it **Simple** and then make it **Compelling**. His problem, made simple, was 71 serious injuries. But why was this so important to address? Where was the urgency? He made it compelling when he boiled it down to the following statement: "We injure on average 1 person every 5 days, compared to the industry standard of 42 days. Any delays in finding and implementing solutions would, on average, result in a major injury every 5 days." This made it URGENT.

Searching for clarity can help you to properly express what it is that you believe regarding the problem you are trying to solve and how it can best be addressed. When everyone has clarity, there is a good basis for shared belief and understanding.

A Project Sponsor should explain the imperatives of a Lean Six Sigma project in vivid terms. Clear alignment of project goals helps ensure the project team is all working towards the same outcome and reduces confusion, which can often result in instability, lack of accountability, poor performance, negative outcomes, and failure. To develop clarity, the sponsor should:

- Set clear organizational priorities and realistic project goals and link them to the Lean Six Sigma roadmap and strategy.
- Clarify the roles and responsibilities of the team members, the executive management, and other stakeholders and ensure acceptance of the project team's ground rules.
- Maintain an effective organizational communication plan.
- Reconcile conflicting personalities and priorities.
- Distil any threat that leads to confusion.

For the sponsor, clarity is the first step to gaining credibility and respect and stamping the project with legitimacy so the team can embrace the shared purpose more readily.

2. Criticality

"A false sense of urgency is pervasive and insidious because people mistake activity for productivity... a sense of urgency is not an attitude that I must have the project team meeting today but that the meeting must accomplish something important today."

– John Kotter (A Sense of Urgency)

The dictionary defines criticality as "the quality, state, or degree of being of the highest importance." In business operations or financial terms, criticality describes the ranking of the severity of the ways in which a system, device, or process can fail, its frequency of occurrence, and the consequences of its failure. This ranking guides organizations in choosing which battles to wage first.

I have had many sponsors who find difficulty in driving the criticality of the project, or as John Kotter calls, "a sense of urgency." As businesses, in my experience, have many opportunities and are constrained only by the availability of critical resources and people to deliver them, I always remind the project team to stress to senior management why the project must be PRIORITISED over others and how the expected outcomes work to achieve organizational goals.

Criticality is all about belief. What do you believe to be critical? What do others consider critical? Get to the bottom of what you should focus on and why, and you will have a good basis for shared belief and understanding.

For Lean Six Sigma projects to succeed, it is important to understand why the organization decided to pursue the initiative. However, a more important concern should deal with the sense of urgency – "the organization should do it NOW, otherwise..." Kotter asserts that:

> "underlying a true sense of urgency is a set of feelings: a compulsive determination to *move and win now.*"

Because feelings are more influential than thoughts, melodramatic stories highlighting urgency are digested with more interest and are embedded in us far longer than high-level presentations or any overly technical explanations.

> The following are the three basic questions that the sponsor should ask team members:
>
> 1. Why is this project more important than all the others, including my day job?
> 2. Why do this project right now?
> 3. What happens if we do nothing?

Making a business case is about taking a *complex* situation and boiling it down to the *simple*. This is often a pivotal question that, if answered, would irrevocably address the aim of the project or initiative. This ability to make it succinct and simple is an iterative process and can take a few hours or even days to get right.

This brings me to the second point around selling the criticality of the project or change – taking the SIMPLE and making it COMPELLING. Just because a senior manager says something does not make it compelling. He must have the ability to sell it as a "story." There is a simple recipe to help sell the criticality against the usual management consultancies' approach of telling the answer first and then selling it as the correct answer. I find this method very effective in making my message both clear and compelling. This process can be done in the following ways:

1. State the current situation the business is facing, e.g., losing market share. Put only the positives from a SWOT analysis in here. State this entity, the aim/mission of the project or initiative, and any preset goals (e.g., x% growth in the next 12 months, reducing capital expenditure requirements, etc.).
2. List all the facts and sort them into groupings relevant to the situation being discussed and put aside irrelevant data.

3. Interpret these groupings and add a sentence – "So what?"

4. Collate the consequences – these can come from a WOT or a SWOT analysis.

5. Create a consequence chain, i.e., a consequence of doing nothing is A, and the consequence of A is B; consequence B produces C, which results as a result of D, and so on. Then, identify root causes – this can come from the analysis phase of a Lean Six Sigma project.

6. Iterate the key or pivotal question and evaluate if the answer accesses the aim of the project or change.

7. Give an answer.

8. Give solutions/recommendations with the supporting data.

> Following this structure tells a story and makes the sale COMPELLING. A simple way to look at this process is to move forward by addressing 5 questions:
>
> 1. Where are we today?
> 2. What needs addressing?
> 3. What questions should we answer?
> 4. How and when are we going to do it?
> 5. Why? (Provide evidence)

To assess the criticality of a certain project, the Lean Six Sigma team must position the vision for the project amidst the spectrum of business challenges, trends, and issues. But this is not enough. To create buy-in for a project, the sponsor should target not only the minds but also the hearts of people to help them feel the urgency.

3. Commitment

"The harder you work, the harder it is to surrender."
—Vincent Lombardi (American football coach)

Commitment, as the dictionary would describe it, is "the trait of sincere and steadfast fixity of purpose or that state of being bound emotionally or intellectually to a course of action or another person or persons." Commitment to a project (including its vision, objectives, activities, and requirements) would then mean belief and acceptance of the project, translated to a willingness to exert considerable effort to achieve goals and purposes and a desire to keep working for the group until completion.

A leader came to seek advice about how he should get his people to "buy into" some Lean Six Sigma proposals. I told him he could go barge in through the front door or creep his way in via the back entrance. Going through the front door would let him visibly demonstrate his vision and actively engage his staff in project planning and implementation. The back door, however, would relegate him to the role of a silent or invisible initiator, policing the changes behind the scenes. He correctly chose the front door.

A Project Sponsor should set the stage for successful project execution by demonstrating confidence, commitment and focus on the Lean Six Sigma initiative. Commitment encourages team members to maximize their skills and use their discretionary energies to learn new things, use new tools, and implement new approaches, which will ultimately enhance collective skill and team ambition.

A project sponsor must also show loyalty to individual welfare because the members can only trust them based on how committed they are to individual integrity and well-being. Sponsors can do this by modeling high-trust behaviors, including accountability and culpability.

Commitment has a lot to do with belief. When people believe that something is worth committing to because they understand the urgency and why it is important, they are more likely to commit. They also need to believe that others are committed too.

In one company I worked with, each sponsor was asked to gather feedback from their team and their Master Black Belt on their performance as a sponsor. One sponsor came very frustrated about the feedback he had from the team and said he needed to discuss the issue as he saw it so he could review it objectively and not hold negative feelings or resentment.

The feedback he had received was that the team did not feel his commitment to the project was high. I asked him what his definition of commitment was, and he said, "I showed my commitment by fully supporting the team, giving them advice and money, answering their questions, and making decisions." I then asked him what he thought the team's definition of commitment was. He answered, the same as his. I asked him if he had asked the team what their expectations were of him as a sponsor at the beginning or anytime during the project. A rather sheepish "No" came as a reply.

We agreed that he should do two things: first, ask his team, in an authentic and non-threatening manner, how he could show his visible commitment, and second, talk to one or two of his peers who felt he had shown commitment and ask how he could do even better in their eyes.

A few weeks later, we spoke again, and he expressed positive enthusiasm about his new skills in eliciting commitment from others and showing commitment in return. One very interesting point is how he reframed the essence of Voice of the Customer: he treated his team members as if they were his customers since he was providing them with a management/ leadership service. He needed to get a VOC and then kept on checking in to see if their needs had changed. This particular sponsor's performance in the employee survey seven months later was the highest ever in the division's history and 9% higher than any other manager.

4. Consistency

*"Make your mold. The best flux in the world will not make
a usable shape unless you have a mold to pour it in."*
—Robert Collier (American motivational author, 1885–1950)

You had a great kick-off meeting with your project team, a signal that the project is off to a great start. Everyone was excited about the project. Each team member was clear about what needed to be done, how to do it and when to do it. After a few days, you take out your checklist and make a cursory evaluation of what has been done so far. To your horror and dismay, not a box has a tick! No one touched or moved anything! If you ask why, you will realize your team has stumbled on several roadblocks. If this can happen at the start of a project, it can happen in the middle and even toward the end.

At each stage of the project, there will always be constraints and unexpected events that bear on the ability to perform such that team momentum and synergy are effectively curtailed. You will realize these stumbling blocks did not all arise from team members. Executive leaders or organizational occurrences cause many project constraints. The importance of consistency right from beginning to end comes to the fore. It is through consistency of efforts and boundless synergy that the project team can hurdle the humps and sidetrack or negotiate events that divert focus.

A leader should show consistency in their words and their deeds. It is walking the talk. Because a successful Lean Six Sigma initiative requires roadmaps, tools, and methods to be used correctly, project sponsors who embrace and strongly espouse the Lean Six Sigma principles will more quickly gain the trust of the project team.

You need to believe in consistency: you need to believe in the importance of following through, and you need to follow through if you want other people to believe in whatever you are trying to get them to do. The relationship between consistency and belief is a close one since people need to see follow-through if they are to invest ongoing time and effort in a project.

Consistency builds trust, trust builds commitment, commitment draws support, support nurtures attitude, attitude bolsters synergy, and synergy enhances success. In this sense, consistency becomes the most pragmatic element of Lean Six Sigma endeavors. As a charismatic leader, the Project Sponsor who consistently expresses their values for Lean Six Sigma generates shared value in the project team.

When I coach sponsors, I never fail to emphasize that they should always imagine themselves as being on stage, the center of attention, the source of inspiration, and the prompt for decision-making and action. Thus, as a sponsor, you have to mean what you say and do what you mean. You have to be "predictable" in that the audience will not doubt your belief and adherence to the Lean Six Sigma project for one second.

Consistency is physical evidence of authenticity and integrity; thus, it is the most effective way to build one's professional brand and value proposition as a sponsor. It is the surest way to sell yourself to your boss and your workforce. Consistency is how the sponsor gains respect and trust from above them and from below. If you have a "now you see, now you don't" attitude to the project, your people cannot grasp your true intentions. They will not know where you are coming from.

And when this happens, fear of uncertainty will creep into the team, or worse, everybody will be led to believe that they can do whatever they want to do in any way they can. But when you consistently show up, speak up, and own up, you can set the tone and tenor of work standards and expectations. Hence, you help the group create consensus, avoid confusion, and maintain project direction.

The sponsor will show consistency and enhance the project's likelihood of success by doing the following:

- Constantly express support for Lean Six Sigma philosophy and values.
- Show consistency between words and deeds.
- Create a coherent and continuous system of identifying and linking opportunities, core processes and the lean Six Sigma roadmap.
- Ensure consistent monitoring of project details and milestones.
- Design a scoreboard to highlight successes, analyze failures and diagnose strengths and weaknesses.

When they can do these, the Project Sponsor creates the mold where their team's productive energies come into shape and are galvanized into fruition and resilience.

Clarity, Criticality, Commitment, and Consistency is a doable paradigm that provides signposts for sponsors in the performance of their job. You may throw in one or more other Cs into the soup, but these 4 Cs should be taken as key ingredients. How to deliver these 4 Cs and how to make them work effectively relies on a set of strategies.

Coaching Framework

Now that we've oriented ourselves toward coaching, let's consider the coaching framework. How can we make sense of our role as coaches? How can we use that understanding to become more effective and more helpful to the people we are trying to coach?

The coaching framework has 6 core dimensions that can be applied both individually and as a whole team. The dimensions are:

- Clarity of **your Role** – are you clear on expectations of your role with your leader and with your team? Are you coaching your team and helping with decisions across your peers and the organization?
- **Your Actions** – Are your actions having an impact that is aligned with the intent? Are they consistent, and are they effective?
- **Your Words** – are your actions having an impact that is aligned with the intent? Are they thoughtful and empowering to others? Are you communicating in a way you are listening and empowering your team and peers?
- **Your knowledge** – Are you continually learning new things? Are you curious and growing both externally and within your team? Are you willing to learn new things with no bias?

- **Your Decisions** – Are your decisions predictable and for the greater good? Are they logical, based on facts and inclusive of other perspectives?

- **Your team** – Are they a team working toward a collective outcome or a group of individuals working on their own goals? Are they aligned and committed?

Figure 5.1 shows these dimensions in the form of a wheel that collectively provides a consistent leadership shadow through 'clarity of thought.'

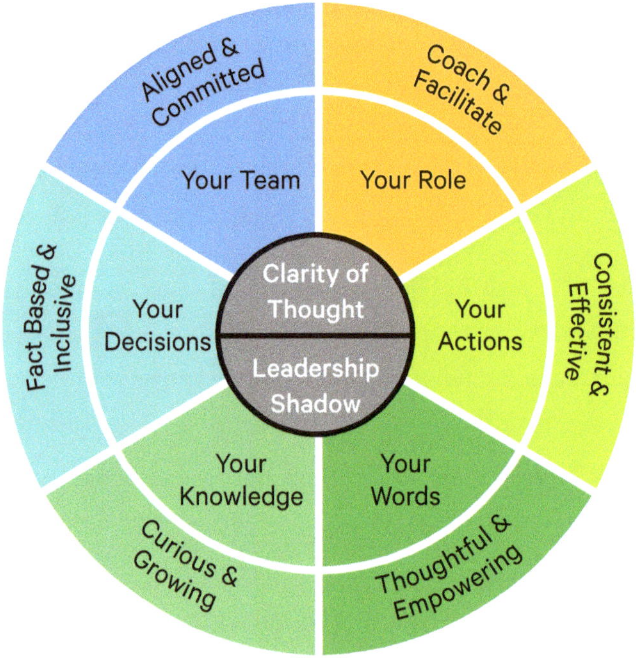

Figure 5.1—The Coaching Framework Wheel (© Action New Thinking)

Your Role

As a Coach

As a leader, my main role is to coach my team to be better every day. I adjust my schedule/*ILO (ILO is "In life off," e.g., day/week/month showing schedule of meetings/routines etc.) to give them quality time and help them realize their growth pathway in the short and long-term. Examples of ideal behaviors for this dimension are:

- I develop my team members.
- I celebrate and recognize my team with enthusiasm.
- I use reward systems to recognize ideal behaviors fairly.

For me, to role model these behaviors, I need to consider my underlying belief for the above to happen: '**Success is letting others develop their ideas and solutions.'**

This means I need to be authentic, and I need to follow the principle of respecting everyone. This is a broad idea with several meanings, but the basic thing to understand is that respect is about something much more than creating a cozy, warm environment in which everyone is nice to everyone else (Jones et al., 2023).

People think respect means "being nice" when it actually means valuing other people—and in this context, we can do that best by giving them adequate tools with which to do their work and a suitable working environment.

More precisely, there are two main kinds of respect we need to model with our actions: general respect for the members of the organization and specific or individual respect for each member, such that they have the feeling that they are valued for what they have to offer the organization.

This means we must create a general climate of respect within the organization by modeling good behavior and helping everyone to grow together. When we do this, we have the perfect environment for fostering individual respect and recognizing and honoring individuals for their contributions to the group's overall success.

Once we understand the central importance of respect, it becomes easier to see what coaching is for. We are not simply trying to teach technical skills, although this may be an important part of our efforts. We are trying to show our employees the importance of valuing our work, our organization, and each other.

We are trying to model an attitude, a fundamental way of viewing the world, that can help us all to succeed together and become more collaborative and innovative.

Sometimes, respecting other people means respecting them enough to tell them where they have fallen short. In order to help a person grow and reach their full potential, this must be done with tact and care. We should also be open to hearing from others regarding our shortcomings and how we can improve.

> (?) Some questions I should ask myself are:
>
> - Am I coaching my people enough to grow their capability?
> - Am I coaching my people to have clarity of their roles and provide clarity to their teams?
> - Am I balancing recognition and hard conversations in a way my team members could unlock their potential?

As a Facilitator

Facilitators serve our organizations and each other. The essential idea here is servant leadership, of seeing one's role in terms of working for the team instead of the other way around (Jones et al., 2023).

Servant leadership, in practice, means that the leader is getting the team focused on how to do their jobs and succeed. A servant leader also asks employees what they think and values their opinions on how to improve the process. Servant leaders provide clear expectations for their employees and help them understand whether they are winning or losing (Jones et al., 2023).

Fortunately, people usually respond well to leaders who show humility as a core characteristic of their leadership style.

A leader who leads with humility is willing to:

- Listen to others: Other people have valuable information and perspectives we need to consider if we are to work together to improve the organization.

- Learn from others: Other people have valuable skills, insights, and suggestions for improvement. Sometimes, they can point out ways we can improve our behavior and help with organizational goals.

- Acknowledge their vulnerability: A basic fact of the human condition is that we all make mistakes and sometimes need to take accountability. A leader who can model this will go much further in earning employee trust than one who does not.

A leader willing to be honest with their employees about their own mistakes will create a space for openness, honesty, learning, and growth. Such leaders can inspire greater dedication because they show a willingness to learn from their errors and shortcomings.

When you show people it is all right to make mistakes, so long as you take responsibility and learn from them, you create a climate in which people can trust each other. Trust is about relying on others to know that they will be responsible for their part of the work and to fulfill their roles within the organization.

Embodying humility and servant leadership is an excellent example of the outward mindset we discussed in Chapter 2. The more you can show people a desire to include them, extend trust, and create shared value, the better.

As a Leader, I manage department resources to enable initiatives my team is developing. I challenge current systems to help with daily work. I help with support from my peers' teams and others in the organization.

- I seek resources to support my team.
- I act as a servant leader.

- I manage systems to take off roadblocks for my team.

For me to role model these behaviors, I need to consider my underlying belief for the above to happen: **'Removing roadblocks helps teams be successful.'**

(?) Some questions I should ask myself are:

- Am I helping with support from other teams to enable my people to deliver and improve?
- Am I helping with timely decisions?
- Am I listening to the feedback and perspectives of others?
- Am I taking accountability for my own mistakes, errors, and shortcomings?

Your Actions

Are Consistent

Your words and actions need to be consistent if people trust you. We all know people who said one thing and did another, and we all know how hard it is to extend trust when it has been badly damaged. Creating an environment in which trust can flourish is one of the most important functions of the coaching role because trust is the basis for performance.

One way to understand how important this is to consider what happens when trust is absent. If some people cannot be counted on to do what they are supposed to do, this has several very pernicious effects:

- It creates inefficiencies: other people must check their work and sometimes even do it for them.

- It creates resentment: no one likes a person who consistently shirks their obligations. We see them as inconsiderate, lazy, and childish. This usually fosters conflict, bickering, and backbiting.

- It incentivizes others to follow their example: after all, if some people are neglecting their duties and getting away with it, why not do the minimum as well?

- It destroys productivity: a climate of work avoidance, resentment, and conflict is toxic not productive.

Leaders who embody a congruence between their words and their deeds can accomplish incredible things. By modeling trustworthiness, they encourage others to follow their example. One encouraging thing to think about here is that, barring a handful of ne'er-do-wells and opportunists, most people genuinely like to be helpful and productive. People *want* to trust others.

No normal, sane person wants to go to work where they can probably shirk many of their duties but at the cost of dealing with petty bickering, in-fighting, and toxicity. This means that if you work to show people you mean what you say and you take actions to back up your words, then most people are likely to respond positively. True, some will take longer than others to come around, and yes, there are exceptions to every rule. Some people will never be pro-social, no matter what—but that's not for most people.

Take the time to create trust in your organization, and you will reap the rewards. Trust matters for all the same reasons a lack of trust does:

- It creates efficiencies: people can trust that their coworkers will be accountable for their roles and their share of the work.

- It creates harmony and camaraderie: most people like being a part of a team that actually accomplishes meaningful things. People in high-productivity teams value, respect, and admire their coworkers.

- It incentivizes others to follow the example set by the leader, and this can help a great deal when socializing new hires. People who join the organization will quickly learn that trust permeates all levels of the organization, and this will encourage them to follow.

- It fosters productivity: after all, when everyone can trust everyone else to do their work, and people enjoy working with their coworkers and trust them, the result will be greater output.

Foster trust based on a foundation of everyone's needs and perspectives, and you'll be astonished at what your organization can do. Become the person people know they can rely on, and they will reward you with their best efforts and their ongoing commitment to improvement.

My team, my peers, and my leaders see me as someone who keeps his word and is responsible for any act.

- I am predictable, and my team trusts in consistency in the way I act.
- My actions model responsibility: I do not shift blame or work onto others, and I take ownership of my role.
- People see that I value them both in my actions and my words.

For me to role model these behaviors, I need to consider my underlying belief for the above to happen: **'Consistent habitual behavior creates culture.'**

> **(?)** Some questions I should ask myself are:
>
> - Are my actions congruent with my words?
> - Am I predictable in my actions?

Are Effective

As a Leader, I work to keep systems simple and effective. Sustainable outcomes through ideal behaviors guide my actions.

Here's a basic truth: People value their time, and they usually respect other people for not wasting it. Show people you will make things as simple and efficient as they reasonably can be, and they will thank you for not needlessly complicating their lives.

- I endeavor to make things simpler for my team.
- I make things as simple as I can without compromising necessary information or functionality.
- I try to eliminate waste, needless complexity, ambiguity, or uncertainty so things can be efficient.

For me, to role model these behaviors, I need to consider my underlying belief for the above to happen: **'Making it easier to do the right thing than the wrong thing.'**

Mistakes in the workplace are often the result of genuine confusion or error, as opposed to laziness or malice. To help steer people toward doing the right thing, take any system and talk to the people who use it.

Ask them where they make the most mistakes. Ask them why they think those mistakes occur and how the system could be redesigned to eliminate or at least reduce them. Ask them, too, about parts of the system that seem to take too much time.

Once you have this information in hand, work to redesign the system so that it will be simpler and easier to use. Work with the people who use the system to make sure that it makes it easier to accomplish the correct thing and harder to make a mistake or commit an error.

> ⑦ Some questions I should ask myself are:
>
> - Am I making it easier for my team to do the right thing?
> - Is the team continuing to make their work simpler?
> - Have we designed the system so it is harder to make a mistake?
> - Is the overall experience of using the system as easy as it can be without compromising the integrity and purposes of the system itself?

Your Words

Are Thoughtful

As a Leader, I pay attention to the way I connect and communicate with people. I try to listen twice of the time as I speak. My words come from thinking what the other hears, not from what I believe I said.

So many misunderstandings happen because people don't take the time to consider how they come across—or what the other person's perspective is. This is where the Outward Mindset is essential: we need to take the time to think about our communication and how we come across to other people.

When we are thoughtful, we think not only about efficiency but also about the perspectives, feelings, thoughts, and needs of other people. We use empathy to understand their perspectives, and where necessary and appropriate, we may also sympathize with them.

Taking the time to be thoughtful is important if we are to be as effective and powerful at communication as possible.

- I care what I say and that others listen and understand.
- I think about other people's perspectives and needs and try to communicate with them.
- I choose my words carefully, depending on the person, the situation, and any ramifying factors.
- I listen to other people so I can get better at being thoughtful.

For me, to role model these behaviors, I need to consider my underlying belief for the above to happen: **'Big ears, big eyes and small mouth, my people can teach me.'**

(?) Some questions I should ask myself are:

- Am I listening to understand or waiting to provide an answer?
- Are my words inspiring the team to improve?
- I manage systems to take off roadblocks for my team.

Are Empowering

As a Leader, I use my word to empower and support my team in the decisions they make. Being empowering is about encouraging people to grow and helping them to feel confident.

The best leaders know how to build up their teams so they can realize more and more of their potential. A leader who manages this will earn the respect, loyalty, and love of their team.

People like a leader who believes in them and inspires them, and they usually reward such a leader with their best efforts because they want to confirm the leader's faith in them, the leader's belief that they can accomplish great and worthwhile things.

Empowering leaders helps their teams to become greater, more productive, more successful versions of themselves. So many people have incredible potential; they need the right combination of knowledge and encouragement to bring it out of them and help them flourish.

As an empowering leader, I approach communication such that:

- I communicate confidently; my team can feel my commitment to them.
- My words offer encouragement and belief: my team can feel I believe that they are capable of great things.
- My words show the way forward and offer inspiration and hope: my team believes that I am guiding them toward something better and greater.

For me, to role model these behaviors, I need to consider my underlying belief for the above to happen: **'Fostering a safe to fail, learn from the failing environment.'**

We all need the chance to learn and grow from our mistakes. We need to try things in an environment in which it is okay to fail.

Of course, we have to ensure that failures do not sink a company—but this is why it is important to allow people to try things in contexts in which they can make mistakes, learn, and grow from them.

Mistakes can be an important part of our growth: we learn not only what to do but why and how to recover from our mistakes.

What we are describing here is resilience: people with the ability to fail and learn from it can get very good at learning because they keep going until they master something. And by making mistakes along the way, they have a better understanding of the lows and the highs.

Properly understood, failure can be a "superpower." If someone can fail and learn from their failure, they can learn how to work at things until they become good at them.

Some questions I should ask myself are:

- Is the 'impact' of my words matching my 'intent'?
- How do I know it is safe to speak up?
- Am I able to communicate confidence and confidently with my team?
- When people make mistakes, are they supported and encouraged to learn from them?
- When people make mistakes, do they learn that making mistakes is part of the learning process?

Your knowledge

I Am Curious

As a Leader, I challenge the way I think. I guide my team to follow scientific methods to solve problems and bring new and innovative solutions to understand and learn from our people.

- I embrace and promote scientific thinking in myself and my team.
- I want to learn from my teams.

For me to role model these behaviors, I need to consider my underlying belief for the above to happen: **'My people know the answers.'**

> (?) Some questions I should ask myself are:
> - What ideas/solutions have my people come up with that I did not think of?
> - What have I learned from my team today or this week?
> - Am I aware of my blind spots?

Am I Growing

As a Leader, I use Gemba's, go & see, and any interaction with my team to learn from them. I give space to my team to strengthen their skills and unlock new ones.

- I want to learn every day, for everybody, with an open mind and no biases.

For me to role model these behaviors, I need to consider my underlying belief for the above to happen: **'Fostering and creating a learning environment.'**

> **(?)** Some questions I should ask myself are:
>
> - What personal biases have I noticed today or this week?
> - What have I learned from my team today or this week?
> - I am aware of my biases and limitations.

Your Decisions

Are Fact-based

As a Leader, I use information and data to make decisions. If I don't know, I go to confirm my hypothesis with my team, and I give them free space to put facts over the table and help them to realize when we are acting by biases.

- I make decisions based on evidence, avoiding acting with bias.

For me to role model these behaviors, I need to consider my underlying belief for the above to happen: **'There are always two sides to a story to understand reality.'**

> ⑦ Some questions I should ask myself are:
>
> - How do I know I have considered all perspectives before making a decision?
> - How much of my decision is based on fact versus experience?

Are Inclusive

As a Leader, I listen and invite others to share their opinions before making any decision. With my team, I embrace and create a safe and respectful environment in which to share their thoughts and beliefs.

- I listen and invite others to share their opinions before making any decision.
- I create a respectful and safe environment for sharing ideas and thoughts.

For me, to role model these behaviors, I need to consider my underlying belief for the above to happen: **'Everyone has a voice and deserves to be heard.'**

> ⑦ Some questions I should ask myself are:
>
> - Have I already made a conscious decision before asking other perspectives?
> - What perspectives from others helped me make an inclusive decision?
> - Was the decision inclusive, and how do I know?

Your team

Is Aligned

As a Leader, I use purpose to inspire my team and be aligned under the same principles and beliefs. My team is aligned by conviction, not by duty.

- I use purpose and vision to inspire my team and be all aligned under the same principles and beliefs.

For me, to role model these behaviors, I need to consider my underlying belief for the above to happen: **'Connection and constancy of purpose is for everyone, and it guides our decisions.'**

Some questions I should ask myself are:

- How do I know my team is aligned?
- How have I verified this?

Is Committed

As a leader, I leave space for my team members to be themselves, building an environment where they can commit between themselves and the organization. My team is committed to the organization and its teams. The commitment is both personal and as a group and aligned to purpose.

- I leave space for my team members to be themselves, building an environment where they can commit between themselves and the organization.

For me to role model these behaviors, I need to consider my underlying belief for the above to happen: **'My people are business owners in their own right.'**

Coaching is the process by which a leader influences other people toward change, directing them to embrace change and helping them to grow in their roles. Rather than imposing a vision, a coach is trying to help their team members see the reason for their vision and see how it can improve the things it is designed to improve. A well-coached team will embrace the coach's vision because they believe in the goal it is designed to address, and they believe that the coach's prescriptions will help get them there. As we have seen, the only way to do coaching properly is for it to be conviction-driven, dynamic, and participative: the coach must believe in what they are doing, and so must the team members. This also means that coaches must understand their team members: they must be able to see things from their team members' points of view and must be able to empathize and make connections to facilitate growth. This is the essence of clarity, criticality, commitment, and consistency: they only work if the coach has a fundamental sense of empathy toward the people they are trying to help and understands the problems that need to be solved if the people are to grow in ways that will help them make continuous improvement in their organization. What you are likely to find is that so much coaching is about a fundamental understanding of human nature: listen to people, ask them to share their experiences, ideas, and concerns, and show them you care, and the relationship will be that much more productive and enjoyable.

> **(?)** Some questions I should ask myself are:
>
> - How do I know my team is committed to our common purpose and goals?
> - How have I verified this?

By now, we've seen that coaching is a process of mentorship in which a leader influences team members toward change. This means that the coaching approach is ideal for the 4+2 Operating System and the 2 Circles Mindset Framework—and vice-versa. What are the 4+2 and 2 Circles frameworks, if not practical roadmaps for a coaching relationship? The whole idea of both of these frameworks is to influence people to adopt better, more productive behaviors that will lead them to continuous improvement. Apply the coaching mentality and the principles of Clarity, Criticality, Commitment, and Consistency to the frameworks, and you're likely to experience incredible results.

An interesting set of principles that can be applied through the coaching process:

- CLARIFY – get an understanding of the current context, reality, and objective.
- VERIFY – look for data to verify the current reality and any blind spots. A Johari Window and Gemba are great tools here.
- AMPLIFY – Amplify the ideal behaviors and beliefs that will improve the situation.

In concluding this chapter, reflect on some of these questions before moving on to the next chapter:

- Am I able to coach and drive understanding of the underlying beliefs to use the operating system?
- Do I understand the link between behaviors and beliefs and coach these to embed the operating system?
- How would I coach myself on my linking beliefs and behaviors and operating system?
- How could I coach the operating system to my organization's context?

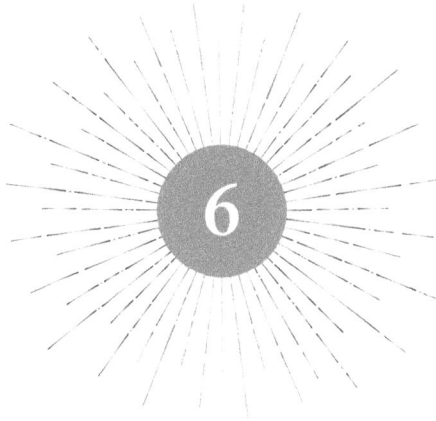

6

Case Studies

In the previous chapters of this book, the mindset framework updated the 4+2 Operating System, and the coaching framework was detailed. Let's look at a few case studies of organizations that have applied some or all of this to their organizations and what the results were. Most of the organizations have asked for anonymity and have not specifically been named.

The following case studies illustrate elements of chapter 3, 4 and 5 being implemented in their organizations:

1. Aged Care.

2. Financial Services.

3. Poultry Farming (Golden Cockerel)

4. Manufacturing and Logistics (Insignia) shows the implementation of the 4+2 operating model.

5. Government Department – Tina Chawner

1. A Christian Aged Care Centre

One interesting example of how to apply the Mindset and Coaching frameworks of the 4+2 Operating System and the integration of the inward and outward circles comes from a local Christian aged care center. The organization is a network of independent local, state, national and international organizations that provide social services in their respective communities. It has a combined income of over $2.28 billion, a workforce of over 21,000 staff and 7,000 volunteers, and the Network delivers more than 50 service areas in the Australian community. This organization uses the belief framework, the 4+2 operating model and the coaching framework. The organization's vision is one of service. Specifically, they define their mission:

> "We exist to support individuals and communities through loving service and sharing hope so that all people live a full life."

In much the same vein, their purpose is:

> "To alleviate poverty and suffering in regional and rural communities by providing integrated and innovative care; and to deliver programs and services to reduce disadvantage among vulnerable and at-risk children, young people, seniors and people living with a disability."

A mere five years earlier, the organization was one of several organizations investigated by the local and federal government, resulting in restructurings to meet minimum regulatory and community standards.

As part of the restructuring and subsequent rebranding, the organization brought in several consultants to help introduce procedures to address the issues. One productivity consultant helped put structures and operating routines in place. This yielded improvements; however, the quality of patient care and staff morale did not improve.

We found that:

- Even though money was spent on improving food for residents, feedback from residents overall was not positive as the focus was purely on nutrition and no consultation with what residents wanted.
- COVID-19 pandemic isolation processes drove a disconnect between care and patient interactions.
- Patients were waiting a long time for a response to a call for help.

Mindset Framework

This situation was ripe for the application of the mindset framework and the 4+2 Operating System. To make the changes, we first worked through developing and defining the vision for the site through workshops with staff, contractors, enterprise leaders, unions, and community groups.

Remember, integrating the outward circle with behaviors behavior, results, and customer satisfaction revolving around outcomes), and the inward circle (beliefs, thoughts, and behavior revolving around mindsets) starts with the outward circle. The basic idea is to improve behavior until you can challenge or build on belief structures and then turn behaviors into unconscious habits. To do exactly this, we came up with:

Vision: Respect Peoples' Life Journeys

Mission: Providing World Class Patient-Centered Care through to the end of life by respecting the whole Medical, Spiritual and Emotional Being.

The organization analyzed the desired behaviors and values, and initially, they came up with a list of five values: Christianity, Compassion, Integrity, Dignity and Inclusiveness.

The key behaviors they identified for these values were Engaging Positively and Respectfully.

We ran into some problems here, however: most of the patients did not share the specific religious beliefs of the organization's leadership. After some rather difficult conversations, we agreed that the other four values provided the fundamentals that should guide the actions of good Christians to provide a respectful environment despite the cognitive impairments of patients.

They came up with a key belief as well: **clients and their families must TRUST us**, and we must show them respect every time, everywhere, every day.

Here, it became clear that they needed to make improvements to bring the reality in line with the ideal. The receptionist was highly stressed and often snapped at other staff and visitors. Focusing on her workload and beliefs helped to overcome the stress she was under. She had a sticker on her computer monitor with two words: "TRUST" and "RESPECT."

Another challenge they had was attracting and retaining staff. This was due to the fact that the aged care industry traditionally pays a minimum salary for front-line staff. One strategy this organization used to meet the challenge was to hire immigrants, but this posed an issue with the language barrier for many of the staff. The language barrier also made for friction between staff and older Australians who had problems understanding them.

One of the most important areas in which the organization progressed was regarding staff showing respect to each other. Over time, they translated this into front-line workers showing respect to the residents and ignoring any inappropriate or rude comments. This helped to generate respect and trust between residents and staff members and made for less friction between them—and this meant lower staff turnover.

Coaching Framework

The organization developed a simple coaching framework that resonated with their enterprise.

Figure 6.1.1—Aged Care Coaching Framework (©Action New Thinking)

Operating System

They took the original model of 4+1 with:

1. Visual Management – they simplified key information about performance for each shift.

2. Huddle – they made sure there was a clear shift handover from day to night shifts, with simple templates and an understanding of what constituted outstanding work.

3. Continuous Improvement – they had a simple 4-step model they implemented based on PDCA (Plan-Do-Check-Act) to solve problems at the right level.

   a. Step One: Explore. Read the problem for understanding. Rephrase the problem in your own words.

   b. Step Two: Plan. What strategy can you use to solve this problem at the root cause?

   c. Step Three: Solve. Solve the problem using your chosen strategy.

   d. Step Four: Check. Is your answer reasonable, and should we adjust it?

4. Standard Operating Procedures – Confirm that the SOP is delivering the desired behaviors and regulatory requirements and lock in improvements to standard work to maintain the improvements.

5. Leader Walks - Teaching leaders to visit with front-line workers to identify opportunities to remove roadblocks. The goal was to help them be more productive and to ensure safety and respect rather than to chastise them for any

missteps. By coaching the workers, leaders fostered trust and alignment.

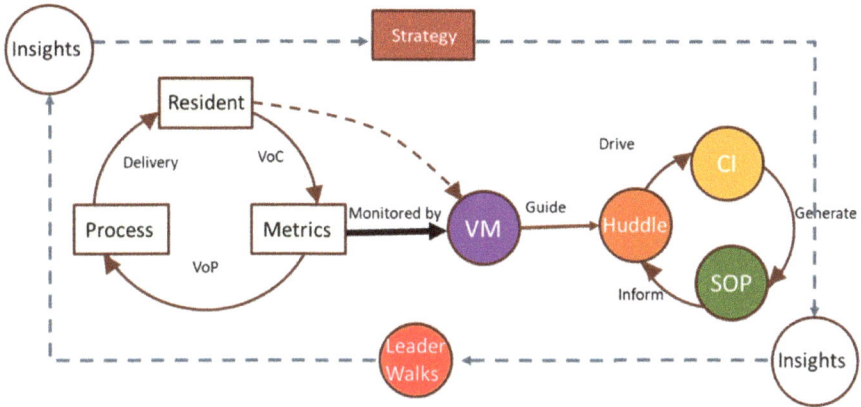

Figure 6.1.2—4+2 Operating System (©Action New Thinking)

In keeping with table 6.1.1 – Beliefs of Operating system, they added a third column aligned to their Christian faith and living life as a good Christian. They asked not to share that material.

	Definition	Beliefs
Visual Management	Habit of continually updating performance data	We understand what value in the eyes of our customers is, so they trust us. It is respectful to have up-to-date data to enable the team to make the best decisions. We use the 1-3-10 rule to drive data transparency and inform the Go and See.
Huddle	Short, sharp performance dialogue addressing gaps and trends	Everyone on the team should know how well things are going, i.e., winning or losing. The team is better at identifying improvements than one individual through Gemba.
Improvement	Enabling teams to fix problems at the root cause within the realm of control.	Improvement is part of who we are. It is done by everyone every day and everywhere in the organization. Working on the right improvements is pivotal to delivering our strategy. We constantly seek perfection and challenge our aspirational targets. We collaborate with all stakeholders to deliver value.
Standard Work	Lock in new improvements and confirm improvements materialized and moving metrics on VMB.	Working as intended and following our processes, standards, procedures, and systems of work will enable us to deliver our strategy and value to the customer.
Leader Walks	Leaders were going to see where the work was done and coach teams to solve the problem where the work was done.	We need to see reality and learn from where the work is done and from those performing the work. We share and communicate the lessons obtained from the Gemba to create value for our people and the customer.

Table 6.1.1—Underlying beliefs of the operating system

Measures of Success

- **Key Performance Indicators (KPIs) – Outcome Measures:**
  » Hours per week with patients.
  » % of volunteer time spent with patients.
  » Average Patient Wait Time for Interaction.
  » Volunteer-to-patient ratio.

» Waiting time from call to patient visit.

- **Key Behavioral Indicators (KBIs) – How we deliver**:

  » Net Respect Score (similar to net promoter score NPS)

  » Collaboration index between Medical and Pastoral care

  » Ability to serve as an example and act correspondingly.

  » Ability to take responsibility.

  » Ability to recognize the achievement of employees.

  » % requests completed on attendance.

2. Financial Services Function in Australia (Written by Steve Dargan)

In early 2019, I had the opportunity to lead a contact center function for one of Australia's largest financial services group companies. This bank was founded in the 1890s and was state-owned until being floated on the Australian SX in the 1990s and currently has over 1.2M customers and 3,200 employees. This case study will focus on the application of the 4+2 Operating System and belief framework.

The business area of focus of this case study is over 300 people across different states. Contact centers are a fast-paced business that attracts the more junior staff to the financial services businesses. These are entry-level roles and ones that most organizations don't necessarily value as much due to the fact they are a large cost base that doesn't drive tangible revenue value for the organization.

That said, it's the most underrated function in an organization. These teams have the unique ability to impact the lives of thousands of the organization's customers daily yet are treated as the "poor cousin" of the organization in general terms. This was something that I noticed when I first took over the function. The business was just "ticking along." The employees had an average engagement score, the customer experience was low, unplanned sick leave was upwards of 18%, and year-one attrition was around 24%. It felt as if they were going through the motions. They had great people and great leaders, but there was a sense of a lack of belief in themselves and where they wanted to be as a business.

One of the first things I did was to get all the 34 leaders offsite for the day to try and tackle a few things so I could get them to believe in themselves and the direction I thought they could go in. We spent the morning mapping out the existing strategy and behaviors evident across each layer of the business, from the frontline to the senior leaders.

The second part of the day was forward-focused. It started with where I believed they could be. I put an aspirational target out to them at the outset. That was *"To be global best in class Contact Centre"* (GBIC). There were a few in the room that you could visibly see get excited. There were others that you could see go, "Yeah, right, that'll never happen." So, I went on to the workshop. What would it mean if we were GBIC? What would it look and feel like? What would our metrics look like if we achieved that?

So, we had an aspirational goal, and we also had measures of success we could track ourselves against each month. The next session I developed was centered around what ideal behaviors we would need at every level of our business. Once we created our ideal behaviors, I got each leader to symbolically "sign them off" so they bought into the new way of working. To finish the day, I had to get them to believe in themselves that they collectively could achieve great things if they all worked with a constancy of purpose. We had a clear vision and a new set of ideal behaviors; however, we needed to all work together to improve the systems to enable the business to achieve our new vision. This led to a **strategy deployment**

session** that I wanted to run. Once we had our goal and the ideal behaviors that would help us achieve that goal, we needed to identify the links between the strategic items we needed to deliver and the tactical initiatives that would assist us in achieving our strategy. Using Hoshin Kanri, we mapped out the key strategic items we needed to achieve to meet our vision. Things like:

- People System improvements
  - » Onboarding and training
  - » Leader development system
  - » Aspiring leader system
  - » Career pathways
  - » Coaching systems
- Work Systems improvement.
  - » Change and Communications
  - » **Visual Management***
  - » **Huddles***
  - » **Standard Operating Procedure***
  - » Workforce management
  - » Reward & Recognition System
- Improvement Systems
  - » Leader Standard work
  - » **Gemba**, or as we call it, looks, listens, and learns walks.
  - » **CI improvement*** & Improvement champion system
  - » 5S

There were still a few non-believers when we left that room; however, it didn't take long for them to change their beliefs when they saw that some of the systems we had changed drove meaningful improvements. One of the most meaningful systems we improved was our People Development system. Before, they were seen as entry-level roles. They weren't seen as a potential nursery of great talent for the rest of the organization. Each team member had the unique ability to appreciate value. We changed the leaders' focus to identifying and enabling each employee to reach their true potential. We changed the leaders' focus from the bog-standard one-to-one discussion to more of a career development discussion. Our leaders were focused on how we grow each capability so they can reach their true potential. This change alone had a dramatic impact on external attrition. We saw our internal attrition increase exponentially, which is a good thing as we knew our system was creating a development pathway for our people with the right values, ideal behaviors and CI focus. We became the "nursery" of great talent for the rest of the organization. Figure 6.2.1 shows the habits we used with PDCA at the center of everything.

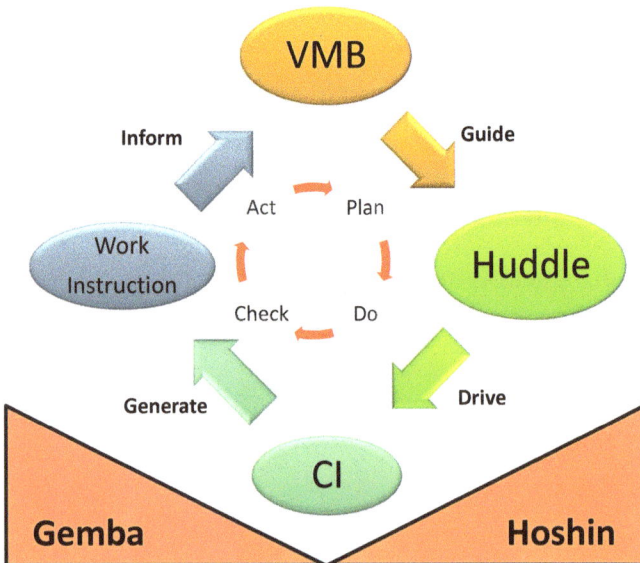

Figure 6.2.1—Our Operating Habits (©Action New Thinking)

When we started to improve this system, we saw our unplanned sick leave reduce and, subsequently, our attrition rate reduce, both of which directly affected our customer experience and performance metrics. The non-believers now believed in where they were heading. They started to "get on the bus" and became advocates for the journey. This system wasn't improved in isolation as each system within the business was highly integrated, so we set about a plan to develop or improve each work, management, and improvement system. Over the next two years, we saw the metrics and customer experience improve month on month. The team started to feel energized that they were heading to GBIC. At the end of the two years, we achieved our GBIC vision, and all our key performance metrics improved (75th percentile). They had a compelling vision, and they all felt they could contribute towards achieving it. They were connected to something higher and more meaningful. They were all rowing the boat the same way. When you get your team to do this, you can achieve amazing results.

3. Printing & Logistics Case Study— Insignia (Written by Evan Powell)

This case study focuses on the implementation of our business operating system within an Operational Team encompassing Production, Supply Chain, and Warehouse. When I assumed this role nearly three years ago, our lead time was 20 days, our on-time performance was in the 60% range, and there was no internal trust in our ability to deliver on our core business requirements within our promises to customers.

As a provider of custom supply chain labeling and traceability solutions, ensuring an exceptional customer experience and seamless delivery is critical to our business. While it is relatively straightforward to focus on external customers, achieving true success requires applying this mindset internally across the business, teams, and individuals.

To illustrate this within the business, we examined the numerous "baton changes" that occur internally, from a customer's initial contact with us to the fulfillment of their order. Much like the 4x400m relay races at the Olympics, where the race is won or lost in baton changes rather than by the fastest individual runners, our internal transitions and overlaps between teams and processes are areas where implementing the 4+2 framework showed significant value for both staff and customers.

The business had a vision or "why"—its reason for being—articulated as "Helping Australia Compete." This vision provided a sense of business purpose, but it was sometimes too nebulous to be effectively understood and embraced by front-line team members, where value creation occurs. By implementing this vision, department leaders had a cause to build visual management systems that would give opportunities to bring this vision to life.

Visual Management

Bringing "Helping Australia Compete" to life was an excellent starting point for introducing visual management. While it is easy to force a top-down approach where managers dictate what should be seen, real value emerges when the team engages and designs in what they need and want to know.

We started with the question, "What do our customers value?" when designing our team boards. The team came back with "Quality, Value, and Responsiveness" as key factors, which were later validated by our sales team and customer surveys. Understanding our customers' needs allowed us to focus on our actions, measures, and, importantly, our team vision: "We Help Australia Compete by making quality products efficiently." This team vision is directly linked to the company vision and resonates with our customers.

We also asked the "Voice of Staff" question: "Why do you choose to work here, and what do you value about working here?" This feedback allowed us to incorporate additional measures and discussion points around Safety, Teamwork, and Behaviors.

In terms of implementing visual management, it is easy to go gung-ho on measures and board layout. However, the most critical aspect of visual management is identifying problems and fostering conversations (huddles) that occur around these issues. It is essential to ensure that the building of a visual management system does not detract from its use. We led with one measure for each deliverable, and each of these had targets and was tracked with causal charts (the Pareto Rule) to guide conversations and future improvement areas.

The below charts show this. The lag measure was Lineal Meters per Hour, which had a target of 1550. To control this, we wanted to increase machine uptime, so we tracked Unplanned Stops – stops that were not tracked to a job. The operators entered the causes for a stop, which allowed us to track on a causal chart and see which stop types were the most overrepresented so we could focus on correcting these areas through improvements and projects.

Dr. Morgan Jones

As we sought to build buy-in to the visual management system and huddles, one clear issue was the team's reluctance to propose new ideas and ways to improve. Common phrases I heard included, "Nothing gets done around here" and "I've asked for it, but I don't know what happened with it," which are all too common in many workplaces.

To address this, I initially arranged sessions with all Production staff across both day and night shifts, along with their line management and support teams. We reviewed the Voice of Customer, Voice of Staff, and Vision and then asked the team, "If this was the best place ever to work, what would it look like?" This was initially met with some laughs, scoffs, and skepticism—they didn't believe this was possible and had never been asked to shape their future before. However, we eventually got some buy-in, with thoughts like teamwork, rewarding work, development, and pay increases starting to emerge. These were surface-level responses, but it was a start.

I then asked, "What are all the things that stop us from being the best place ever to work?" Ideas and suggestions following this question were more forthcoming and, better still, tangible and actionable. To set the priorities for these, we gathered the whole team a week later and placed the ideas on a PICK chart. It was made clear to the team that we wouldn't be able to complete all the ideas immediately, but we would commit to focusing on all the high-value, easy-to-implement ideas and continue to recalibrate the priorities with the team. The team determined what they deemed low or high value and what was easy or hard to complete—and, importantly, who should do it.

The next step was to make these ideas visible and actionable. We introduced a visual project board to track and manage these projects. All committed but unassigned projects sat in "The Hopper," and projects to be worked on were assigned to a team member with a timeline of This Week, Next Week, This Month or Blocked.

This made it easy to see what the team was working on and what was upcoming. Anyone could add a new project or suggestion to The Hopper. It would then be prioritized and assigned in a huddle. Different colored post-it notes were utilized based on the type of work required: Safety, Maintenance, Productivity, etc. This visual management system made it easy to see what improvements individuals were working on, what type of improvements and if anyone was overburdened.

While it is easy to paint this as a way of getting everyone's problems resolved easily, the reality is that with any system to manage improvements, things don't always get done in the committed timeframe. Other priorities arise, problems are more complex than anticipated, or other work takes precedence. To drive accountability simply and effectively, if an improvement wasn't completed in the committed timeframe, that post would get a "/" added to it. At this time, we would ask the owner if they were still able to complete it and when it would be completed. If they reached "///"—no, it wasn't three strikes and out—the individual would buy the team a morning tea of their choice. This approach enabled us to maintain focus on performance, communication, and transparency while also keeping an empathetic, human element in our processes.

An essential part of creating consistency and performance around huddle boards was training leaders to facilitate huddles effectively. Part of this effective facilitation was for them to reach the point where the team owned the huddle, and the leader could participate rather than facilitate. Traditionally, huddles are based on power dynamics where the leader provides information. The way we need to run huddles is focused on team members leading, as they have more information about the work and value creation, and the leader learns to listen and ask probing and clarifying questions to focus on the right areas.

Strategy Deployment

To facilitate the delivery of our vision, the leadership team developed our mantras, which were rolled out across the business on a company-wide strategy day. The mantras are:

- Simplify the Process
- Deliver Exceptional Service

- Find a Safe & Sustainable Way
- Everyone Sells Everything
- We are Always Better Together

At the strategy day, we facilitated conversations in cross-functional teams to identify "mechanisms" or ideas within each mantra for the business to focus on in the coming year.

To underpin our rollout of the Mantras, we implemented a Mantra Mover & Shaker Award—a baton. This ties back to the relay race analogy mentioned earlier. The term "baton change" became a ubiquitous saying within the business, emphasizing collaboration and cohesion among our teams. We introduced a physical baton award as a symbol for a team member who went above and beyond to bring a mantra to life.

While the rollout of these mantras and the strategy deployment went well, there were areas for improvement. In the months following the strategy launch, the mantras became well-understood and regularly communicated by team members. However, execution, focus, and delivery of the strategy were identified as areas needing improvement.

Strategy Execution and Improvements

This is where better utilizing and training in Standard Work and Leadership Walks would have been exceptionally beneficial to the business. We developed strategic, operational plans on A3s in conjunction with functional teams, but a consistent focus on working through these documents and their deliverables was lacking.

In reflection, we had implemented visual management and huddle routines well in individual areas but not consistently across leadership teams and their functional areas. We were operating with disparate systems, not a standard operating system. This resulted in leadership huddles, often turning into reporting sessions rather than decision and action-focused sessions to remove roadblocks. Consequently, while we achieved agile delivery of improvements in functional areas, issues escalated to the leadership level and often got stuck with communication not flowing back down easily or transparently.

Another underutilized part of this framework was standard work. Attempting to implement standard work across a team was often seen as micromanagement. While making tasks visible drives accountability, we struggled to sell the benefits of habit, consistency, and predictability in completing work. We are currently working with our production team to reimplement this with a focus on "Jobs to be Done" on a daily, weekly, and monthly basis, following some process changes where things have been missed.

To underpin future success, developing and focusing on our leadership capability to hold meaningful, inquisitive conversations with their teams is critical. Leaders walking through the business and discussing the work being completed bring immense value to all parties. So far, we have done this on an ad hoc basis. Even with this informal approach, the benefits have led to national safety improvements and advancements in waste management and sustainability.

Our plans to formalize this process involve partnering a senior leader with a mid-level leader in the business on a rotational basis. The purpose of the senior leader is to demonstrate the desired behaviors and coach the mid-level leader to develop their capability. We need to ensure that staff conducting these walks ask the right questions in the right way. A clear, empathetic introduction and a request for permission are fundamental to building respect. From there, entering a conversation with open questions—ranging from what they are working on to what problems they are encountering to what changes they would make—can all offer valuable insights.

This process of implementing an operating system has taken place over nearly two years. It has not been perfect, but it has certainly had its learnings for all involved. However, we now have an operating team running to a 10-day lead time with a 96% on-time performance and a much more engaged workforce, though there is still room for improvement.

This case study focuses on the implementation of our business operating system within an Operational Team encompassing Production, Supply Chain, and Warehouse. When I assumed this role nearly three years ago, our lead time was 20 days, our Delivered in Full, On Time (DIFOT) was in the 60% range, and there was no internal trust in our ability to deliver on our core business requirements within our promises to customers.

As a provider of custom supply chain labeling and traceability solutions, ensuring an exceptional customer experience and seamless delivery is critical to our business. While it is straightforward to focus on external customers, achieving true success requires applying this mindset internally across the business, teams, and individuals.

To illustrate this within the business, we examined the numerous "baton changes" that occur internally, from a customer's initial contact with us to the fulfillment of their order. Much like the 4x400m relay races at the Olympics, where the race is won or lost in baton changes rather than by the fastest individual runners, our internal transitions and overlaps between teams and processes are areas where implementing the 4+2 framework shine, adding significant value for both staff and customers.

The business had a vision or "why"—its reason for being—articulated as "Helping Australia Compete." This vision provided a sense of business purpose, but it was sometimes too nebulous to be effectively understood and embraced by front-line team members, where value creation occurs. By implementing this vision, department leaders had a cause to build visual management systems that would give opportunities to bring this vision to life.

4. Poultry Farming—Golden Cockerel (Written by Bob Carter)

Seeing Is Believing

The Golden Cockerel Group is comprised of several companies involved in poultry processing in the state of Queensland. The Group markets and distributes a range of both fresh and frozen poultry products to customers throughout Queensland, Australia, and the international market. Golden Cockerel Pty Ltd was formed in 1972 and is owned jointly by two families, the Benefits and the Elks, who have been involved in the poultry industry for three generations. The Group is fully integrated and comprises feed mills, hatcheries, parent farms, broiler farms, processing plants, and distribution. The facilities are well spread and isolated from a disease control viewpoint in order to ensure continuity of supply in times of adversity.

The secret to success has been the capability of the senior management to believe in what they are doing and why this is important. They needed the following three conditions to be met to be successful.

1. They needed to be **Ready** for change. They needed a reason to change and had to prepare themselves and their teams for it. They needed to create a vision for the future.

2. They needed to be **Willing** to adapt. This includes learning from failures and successes and the persistence to keep going despite setbacks.

3. They needed to be **Able** to change. This means ensuring that sufficient resources are made available to support the program – people, finance, time, materials, etc.

Henry Ford is quoted as saying:

"'If you think you can do a thing or think you can't, you're right.'"

The difference is what you believe you can do.

Continuous Improvement programs should never be tool-driven. CI tools such as visual management, 5S, Huddle Boards, etc., should always be enablers and used when the organization is ready to adopt them. As a seasoned CI practitioner, I have always completed a "Readiness Survey" before designing a Continuous Improvement program for an organization. As the old saying goes, "One size does not fit all."

Furor, a New Zealand-based beverage company, met all three conditions, believed in what they were doing and was prepared to trust the process when implementing a Continuous Improvement program across their processing sites. They met with outstanding success. Within three months of commencement, they had over 1,000 improvement ideas, and Henk Roling (Manufacturing Director) stated, "It is like someone has turned a light switch on." The floodgates of change had opened. The biggest change was for the leadership team, which had to adapt and learn how to channel the newly created energy.

More recently, I have been working with Golden Cockerel, a poultry processor based in Queensland, Australia. They started with a CEO and consultant-led journey but failed to engage with some of the senior and middle management and get them on board – they were not believers.

After several value stream mapping exercises and the development of standard work and huddle boards, the team was disillusioned and had endured several false starts. The CEO, Operations Manager and several supervisors decided to move on to new opportunities.

A new operational structure was put in place, and the new management and supervisory teams quickly created a new set of values and ways of working within the company. The focus becomes passion, care, adaptability, growth, and dependability. A new operational cadence was formed, leading to a realignment of team focus and accelerated performance.

Within three months, the culture of the company had changed. People were on board, and the energy within the company was changing. Minor modifications were made to processes and equipment, and performance started to improve. People now started to believe in themselves again and were prepared to implement change. With belief comes empowerment, the key to engagement at all levels.

Golden Cockerel now hosts "Best Practice" visits to share their journey with others through their partnerships with the Best Practice Network and the Association for Manufacturing Excellence.

At the time of writing, Golden Cockerel is still on a journey of continuous improvement. Using the 4 + 2 Operating system, most of the habits are in place and starting to work really well. Let's explore what has worked and some of what has been learned.

Habit 1—Visual Management Habit

This is an area that needs more work as most Visual Management systems are electronically based and hidden from most users. The huddle boards include "Improvement Opportunities" and "Action" sections. Our challenge is to make these more visible in the workplace and use them to drive change.

This starts at the top as the leadership team is good at strategy planning, and whilst working hard on strategy deployment, this could be significantly enhanced with the regular use of Visual Management systems and developing the habit of regular review. There is definitely more work to do to develop this habit.

Habit 2—Huddle Habit

Individual Huddle Boards that were created by the teams following a consultant-led workshop were totally redesigned, and a standard template was developed to ensure consistency between teams with like processes. Team leaders and supervisors now attend Huddle Board meetings in other sections to learn and share best practices. Bespoke operational and support service areas modified the base design and customized their own boards to suit their operations while retaining the common focus.

The new emphasis at the daily huddle board meetings became identifying a "Golden Cockerel Moment" (where good things are shared between departments – new records, someone or a team going beyond expectations) and finding someone who had done a "Good Job" - they were then nominated for a weekly recognition reward. Reinforcing good behavior results in more of them and reinforces belief in what you are doing.

With the introduction of Power BI as a software platform, several of the Visual Boards are now complemented by digital versions providing real-time data comparisons with target measures.

The huddle boards have become a key focus of each of the shifts on start-up and are manually updated during the production process with performance metrics. They have become a key focal point for all teams and different functional layers within the business.

Habit 3—Continuous Improvement Habit

Golden Cockerel is still developing a bottom-up "Improve Everyday" culture. While many are on board, high employee turnover and the ethnic makeup of the workforce make this a challenge throughout the business. With a new leadership team in place, this is starting to change as people become empowered to follow through with their ideas. Another challenge is resourcing the changes as we put more strain on our maintenance, engineering, and quality assurance teams to assist with the implementations required. This has led to an increase in staff numbers in the support roles, further improving our capabilities and processes.

Habit 4—Standard Work Habit

Being in the food industry means lots of audits, and every auditor wants to ensure that our processes are being consistently followed – this is something that Golden Cockerel does really well. Work instructions are regularly reviewed based on their importance to the business and updated following any changes. Training records are kept, and staff are retrained as soon as possible after any changes occur.

Regular huddle board communications, toolbox talks and one-point lessons supplement work instruction training.

Habit 5—Leader Walks Habit

Leader Walks are yet to become a regular habit for all leaders, as some will only undertake a Leader Walk when they have a purpose. Our better leaders incorporate their Leader Walks into their daily activities, developing deeper relations with their teams (building respect and trust) and increasing their understanding of the processes and challenges that their teams are engaged in.

Habit 6—Strategy Deployment Habit

As mentioned previously, strategy planning is a strength of the leadership team, whilst the current weakness is the monitoring and review of the deployment strategy.

This is currently tracked using a spreadsheet that is made available to each of the leadership teams for regular updates. If one team member fails to update the spreadsheet, few will be aware as it is not discussed on a regular basis within the team. There is a massive opportunity here simply to develop a cadence of review and implement a "Team Retrospective" of the process to develop buy-in and increase the visibility of progress.

Current State

Golden Cockerel is well and truly on its Continuous Improvement journey. In the last six months, it has been a finalist in the Food Industry Association of Queensland (FIAQ) "Manufacturer of the Year" Award and the Queensland State Training Awards – recognition by external parties further reinforcing the results and creating more believers within the organization.

When you have the chance to take advantage of "Best Practice" visits and "Study Tours," you will soon learn what believers already know – how to lead and implement a continuous improvement journey whilst engaging with your teams. Leverage the ideas and concepts back into your organization to accelerate your own implementation journey further.

Don't underestimate the power of sharing best practices with other organizations, leverage their experience and "Go See" – seeing is believing.

5. Belief in a Government Department—Transforming Through Emotional Connection and Drive (Written by Tina Chawner, Yellow Hat Consulting)

We work with executives who are looking to change or transform their organizations. This can be anything from introducing new IT to changing an operating model. Most of the time, to truly transform, they need to change most aspects of their businesses, from culture through to technology, to some extent. Our approach combines change management, strategic communication and collaborative co-design. This unique approach enables leaders to win hearts and minds and drive change fast.

As an example, we were working with an organization that needed to reduce the cost of their operations, urgently raise capital and improve the satisfaction of their customers and shareholders. The organization was complicated. They had multiple stakeholders, the customers were varied, and they had over 500 employees who had a range of different skill sets to deliver the services.

The executives knew the scale of the change was significant, and they were committed to leaving a legacy. We were asked to provide change management support to help them through the change. As Morgan points out at the start of this book, any transformation starts with understanding the health of the organization. We immediately began scanning to learn about their context, the maturity and health of different aspects of the organization, what was driving the change, and how leaders and staff felt about the change. It became apparent the leaders were not fully aligned on the reasons for the change or their vision. We needed them to connect not just practically but at an emotional level and to imagine what the future could look and feel like for them, their people, and their customers.

As John Kotter stated in 'The 8 Steps to Leading Change,' the first step is to create a sense of urgency, a guiding coalition of support and a vision. However, they needed to move quickly, so we had to act fast and win their hearts and minds.

We brought together around 45 of their team, reconfirmed their purpose, and let people explore why they were passionate about what the organization delivers. The energy in the room was incredible, the buzz and excitement, and, most of all, the passion. It was the type of energy that made the hairs on your arms stand up!

Then, as part of the session, we invited customers to share their experiences. We facilitate many of these sessions as we help organizations kick-start their journeys. The sessions that have the most impact are always the ones where we bring in an external voice, a customer, to hear from the source. It often takes bravery from leaders to invite customers into the room. You don't know what they will say. They may criticize the services currently offered. In my experience, over many years, customers are always delighted to be invited. They are honest and constructive and want to support organizations in improving. On this occasion, the customers delivered a mix of messages about the things the organization does well and areas in which they feel improvements could be made, but their comments were made with such passion and desire that they resonated with everyone in the room. The debrief of this session was critical. As Morgan states, 'We like change, especially when it's for the better.' We facilitated a conversation using coaching questions to help them explore what the messages from the customers meant for the organization and what it meant for them so they could identify the 'better future.'

Then comes the fun part: learning from other organizations that have transformed and succeeded in understanding the art of the possible and using this as input to dream about their future. Seeing an organization that has changed is always inspirational; it demonstrates that it can be done and can ignite ideas. Also, when you let people explore the problems for themselves and the potential solutions, you bring together their subject matter expertise, outside perspectives, and a frame of thinking that allows solutions that would otherwise never have been discovered.

When we facilitate co-design sessions, such as this one, we apply the methodology of MG Taylor, a powerful collaborative co-design approach.

> "The core of the Taylor Method is the integration of the physical environment, work processes and technology augmentation to facilitate human creativity and GroupGenius®. With this method, learning, design, and productive work are integrated. Work processes are human-focused and compatible with the organization that supports them. ValueWeb® architecture is the primary organizational ecology." (Source: https://www.matttaylor.com/public/mgt_tool_kit.htm)

Every aspect of a codesign session is considered to achieve a breakthrough in mindset change and solutions. Some of the ideas would be a stretch to be immediately actioned, and others could be implemented quickly. But what they had was a sense of urgency, a coalition of support and a vision for their future.

We helped them articulate their vision and the approach to deliver on this vision, but most importantly, they shared their passion and beliefs. The communication with staff was planned and coordinated to create the maximum energy and excitement to drive change. The plan was to communicate with all leaders first. However, we know that for someone to buy into a vision and its beliefs truly, they must feel part of its creation. It wasn't good enough for the leaders to simply present and take a few questions.

We designed interactive conversation sessions with the leadership team in small groups. The critical ingredient that always makes these engagements successful is the coaching we provide, both informal and formal coaching. Throughout designing the session and preparing the leaders for the interactive conversations, we were coaching and asking them to explore what success looked like, what behaviors they wanted to drive, and, therefore, what they felt they needed to do.

Before each employee session, we met with each leader for formal coaching. During the conversations, we explored different perspectives together. We weren't the owners of the content or the conversations, so they needed to lead the discussions, but we provided coaching questions to help them explore. Early on in the coaching discussions, we will ask a key question:

'After you have finished the conversation session with your managers, what does success look like to you?'

The leaders were consistent; they wanted their staff to not only understand the vision but to own it, and they wanted their managers to lead the change, be proactive and implement change. We therefore recommended a coaching approach to the conversation session. As Morgan stated earlier, 'coaching does not mean imposing one's vision but facilitating the opportunity for team members to accept and embrace your vision.'

We then explored ways to achieve this goal with leaders. This meant the leader needed to play the role of facilitator and coach during the discussions. We then explored the role they wanted the managers in their teams to play during and after the conversations. From our evaluation of the health of the organization, we knew this was a change in the style of leadership. To support the leaders, we provided examples of questions they could ask themselves and their staff as a cheat sheet. Here are some of those questions.

Questions to ask yourself to check if you are actively listening:

- How much talking are you doing?
- Are you present and focused on just this discussion?
- Validate what has been shared:

>> Thank you for sharing that

>> Respond thoughtfully and consider asking them to 'tell me more.'

Empower by asking questions

- Can you tell me more about that? (One of my favorite questions to ask during coaching and facilitation conversations. Even if I understand, it's a great way to explore further and check what assumptions I've made, and I always feel I learn something new by asking this simple question.)
- What trends are you noticing?
- What is not working?
- Where do you think we need to start?
- What should we all focus on?
- What does great look like for you and your team?
- How do you think you can best support these changes?
- What do you need from me?
- What do you think could prevent our success together?
- What will you do with what you learned today?

Some of the leaders asked us to listen to the conversations, and if they slipped back into providing solutions, we would remind them of the open questions they could use to encourage their managers to explore and own the solutions.

Now, we had the leaders and managers onboard, and the hard work was about to start! The organization needed to implement the change and to do that, it needed to keep its passion and belief in the vision alive continuously. The leadership regularly checked in on their progress.

The context for the organization would change, just like it does for every organization. However, they revisited their articulation of the story and vision, reset the context and provided opportunities for managers to explore how this affected, or didn't affect, their vision. They shared with people what they had achieved and what they needed to focus on next.

Throughout the changes, this organization has kept its vision and its people's connection and passion for the vision at the heart of everything they are doing. The results of their employee pulse survey dramatically increased. For instance, in 2021, only 26% of employees responded positively to a question about 'in my agency communication between SES and other employees is effective,' and by 2023, the result was 45% positive. During this time, they made remarkable changes across their operating model, the way they provide services and their IT and infrastructure.

It isn't always easy to make space to explore and take time to align with the vision, the context, and what this means for us. However, when leaders make space for themselves and their people to connect practically and emotionally, they accelerate their ability to drive towards it fast.

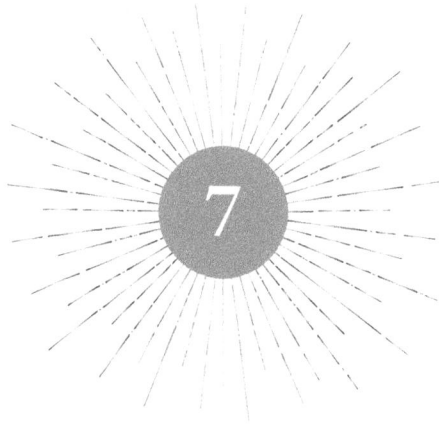

7

What Next?

Throughout this book, I have discussed the outer circle and the inner circle and how we bring these two circles together to form strong behaviors through underpinning beliefs. I have introduced a coaching framework and a proven enterprise excellence model (4+1), which I evolved to an updated 4+2 model. We have discussed how these insights are relevant through several case studies involving various organizations. So, this raises the question: what next?

Let's start with one of the more obvious answers: now you can go forth and *implement* everything we've talked about in this book. I believe in these ideas because I have developed them through rigorous field testing or encountered them in the world—and I know that if you try them, you'll see them work for you.

I hope that I've supported not only what to do but also why, and we've touched on the how as well. With any luck, you're converted, or at least willing to give these ideas a shot and see if they work as advertised. But the proof is in the pudding, as the saying goes, and so it's worth our while to talk not only about *What, Why,* and *How* but also about the question of *How we can start.*

So, how *can* you start? As we've seen, the answer can be found in the inner circle definition:

1. +1 Leader Walks (Gemba) Habit - As the architect of change, start with the behaviors you want to see and hear at all levels.
2. Align these behaviors to the organization's values, i.e., the behaviors that bring to life the values.
3. Work through what needs to be true for these behaviors to be true, i.e., what must people 'believe' to enable these behaviors as something they want to do rather than enforced on them, i.e., compliance.
4. Crystalize the thinking to align values and beliefs.

From there, you can move on to the outer circle:

5. Simplify the strategy and define deployment to a level that front-line workers understand how their daily work contributes to team > department > division/asset > organization strategy delivery. An X-matrix is a powerful tool to help with this.
6. [VMB] Define a simple set of KPIs and KBIs, ideally leading or a mix of leading and lagging. (Transform Behaviors Transform Results – Jones, Butler, and Plenert).

7. [VMB] Clarify the Visual Management Board and how you want it to be used. i.e., what behaviors do you want it to drive, e.g., what conversations do you want to have the VMB drive and identify opportunities for CI, Gemba, field leadership etc?

8. [Huddle] Ensure the purpose of the huddle is clear, and set a simple agenda to help keep the time to 10-15 mins max.

9. [CI] Ensure the gaps identified in the VMB metrics have a structured approach to solve and know how you will track the impact.

10. [SW] Ensure improvements are locked into standard work/ procedures and impact is being tracked for several months.

11. [4 Habits] Ensure training is set up to drive this improvement engine.

12. [+2 Leader Habit] Make sure Gemba is built into the leader's standard work and that leaders reflect on their lessons. WILO/MILO are great tools to help here (WILO is a week in the life of, and MILO is the month in the life of and a summary of meetings, routines, one-on-one visits, etc.).

Finally, verify the experience of staff is actually generating the right beliefs to drive results (see section 7.5 for more details). The key thing is not to start the process with the "WHY," as Simon Sinek would suggest. Instead, start with the overall design, then build the "muscles" of improvement through the first four basic habits, thus creating "muscle memory."

From there, use the +2 leadership habits to reinforce and support the four basic habits, and then go on from the outer circle to the inner circle. Once you're there, you'll be ready for the "Why," i.e., the underlying beliefs and how they link to values, both at the personal level and the corporate level.

You might use a personal leadership change story to show vulnerability and humility and to demonstrate empathy.

One thing that must be understood here is the importance of empathy and empathic leadership, which are very much outcomes of the 4+2 schema and the positive application of coaching and mentorship. Empathy is the ability to cognitively model or understand the world from another's point of view—not to be confused with sympathy, which is the emotional experience of feeling for someone and which has its own importance. It is common for people to confuse empathy with sympathy, but in many respects, empathy is more important for a leader because it lets the leader see the world through the eyes of others, even and especially when a leader does not sympathize with them.

With that said, empathy can help you have sympathy for others, and it is important in leadership because it will help you help other people. Empathic leaders are more likely to be sensitive to signs of overwork in other people and to show interest in their needs, hopes, and dreams. They are more likely to want to help employees with personal problems and convey compassion where it is called for. Overall, empathic leaders can better understand what their employees need, and they can better deliver it.

Employees are, as a rule, quick to learn whether their leaders are empathic, and they respond. Empathic leadership seems to be correlated with meaningful increases in job performance, as Gentry, Weber, and Sadri (2007) discuss in their white paper, Empathy in the Workplace: A Tool for Effective Leadership. While there are cross-cultural differences, there appears to be real evidence that leaders who show empathy encourage greater effort and engagement from their employees.

Shingo Model Approach

Character is important for establishing trust, but once we have trust, what do we do with it? The answer is that we need to take that trust and invest it in creating a high-performance culture that will support continuous improvement—after all, that is what we are trying to accomplish. By meeting this goal, we will reward our employees with a culture that offers them a strong sense of mission, purpose, empowerment, and accomplishment.

So, how do we create that desired culture? One of the more compelling attempts to answer this question comes from the Shingo Model, a formula for success that requires us to define the desired culture, which we accomplish through Guiding Principles, beliefs that become the yardstick by which all behaviors are measured. The external world measures us by looking at KPIs (Key Performance Indicators). However, these are not transferable or relatable to the employees who do the work. They need metrics that guide them and define what direction they should move. They need KBIs (Key Behavioral Indicators). These metrics help employees define their direction and goal. They motivate correct responses—and over time, they help to change employees' beliefs.

KBIs are incorporated into the systems required for any organization to achieve enterprise excellence. These systems are integrated into other systems, all motivating the organization's behaviors towards its Guiding Principles, the beliefs that serve as its True North and help to motivate ongoing improvement.

Tools like Lean and Six Sigma are also vital for creating systems that can help an organization achieve change in keeping with the beliefs that form its Guiding Principles. There are over 100 tools in the Toyota Production

System (TPS), of which Lean and Six Sigma are a couple. The Change Manager will identify the correct tool for any improvement project.

With the correct systems in place, using the best KBIs as behavioral and motivating metrics, which are focused on our goal-setting Guiding Principles, we have started ourselves down a journey toward Enterprise Excellence.

Self Reflection and Building Habits

Once we have the correct systems in place and are working toward enterprise excellence, how can we make sure we stay on track? The answer lies in self-reflection and a commitment to building and maintaining good habits. With self-reflection, we can see ourselves: what we are doing, what we are not doing, what is and is not working and how to improve.

We're talking about learning, and learning is a real skill. We are all taught things, but we are not taught *how to learn*. The benefits of learning faster are forever ending:

- Higher Working Performance
- Greater Opportunities
- More Productivity
- Less Stress

Here are a few techniques to build habits by learning better:

1. Spaced Repetition - Learn consistently over time.
2. The 80/20 Rule - Focus on the 20% that generates 80% of results.
3. The Feynman Technique - Learn things by simplifying them.

4. Study at 2X Speed - Watch/listen to the material at 2X speed.

5. Use Multiple Resources - Get more parts of your brain firing; use books, audio, or videos.

6. Write Things Down - Retention improves when things are written down.

7. Test Yourself - Recall knowledge and identify weak points, have fun and create a quiz with colleagues.

Improve your learning speed and improve your learning retention. Watch your life improve around you.

More Questions About the 4+2 Operating Model and Coaching Framework

Leading with questions shows the leader understands they don't have all the information and they value others' perspectives. Asking questions benefits uncovering insights, perspectives, and challenges before deciding on what is needed from them to serve the situation best.

1. Questions To Understand Other Perspectives

The best leaders value that people bring different experiences, values, goals, and perceptions, which leads to a more holistic understanding of the issue.

- What is working? / What is not working?
- What do you feel I need to understand better?
- What does success look like? / How important is this to you?
- How are you doing during this challenging time?

(?) **2. Questions To Generate Solutions**

The transition to generating solutions is the most satisfying part of the conversation because the leader is now partnering with others to develop viable solutions. This is the part of the conversation where the work of listening to all perspectives can pay off with new insights and buy-in for action.

- What should we do next?
- What is the biggest obstacle, and how can we overcome it?
- What support do you need from me and others?
- What actions should we plan to take next?

Important: Taking time to ask questions to understand the situation better doesn't stop leaders from sharing their needed perspectives; it just means they choose to ask questions to better understand others' views before sharing their perspectives.

Measuring Success

Measuring the mindset framework and operating system is something to consider. There are two key measures I talk about extensively in my book *Transform Behaviors, Transform Results*:

1. Results or Outcomes: Organizations use Key Performance Indicators (KPIs) like volume, cost, quality, and customer satisfaction.

2. Culture: Organizations usually use employee satisfaction surveys. High-performing organizations use Key Behavioral Indicators (KBIs).

A colleague challenges KPIs as mere performance indicators and says they should be reframed as "Keep People Informed" as a leading indicator and "Keep People Inspired" as the lagging indicator.

Key Behavior Indicators (KBIs) can be sustained in ways that turbocharge your organization, and there's one simple trick to doing it: reward good behavior and manage bad behavior. In my book, I talk about many angles to doing this, but for this post, I will highlight one.

KBIs are not simply Key Performance Indicators (KPIs) that measure people. KBIs help you to select, measure, and optimize behaviors that support your organization's values, brand, strategy, and purpose and build your organizational culture.

Selecting a good set of KBIs and leading from the top without exception is a great way to stop behaviors you don't want. Rewarding the behaviors that make up the KBIs doubles down on this and reverses negativity.

How do you do it?

It is difficult and can be confronting for a lot of leaders, but once established as "how we do things around here," it becomes a treasured part of what makes people stay and perform like never before.

Final Thoughts

The whole essence of operational excellence is to empower people and to empower them truly, and they need to believe they are empowered. Consider answering this simple list of questions as the next steps:

1. What are the consistent behaviors in our front-line people needed to deliver sustainable results?
2. What do front-line people need to 'believe' to do the desired behaviors all the time?
3. What do the front-line experiences need to be to reinforce the right beliefs?
4. Are the leader's actions creating the right reinforcing front-line experiences to reinforce the behaviors?
5. What do the leaders need to believe to do 1-4 above?
6. How are you regularly going to verify 1-5 above?
7. How are you recognizing 1-6 above?

Hopefully, this book has given you insights into the importance of the underlying beliefs in building behaviors to deliver sustainable results.

I remember being told a story years ago about a leader walking through a construction site. She meets a bricklayer and asks him what he is doing, and his answer is simple: "I'm laying bricks." The leader walks on further and comes across a second bricklayer and asks the same question, but the answer is slightly different: "I am building a wall." The leader walks on and meets a third bricklayer and asks her what she is doing. The answer came back with passion: "I'm here building a cathedral." There's a similar story about John F. Kennedy asking a cleaner at NASA what they did, and the surprising answer was, "I'm here to put a man on the moon." Beliefs can drive people to do extraordinary things because they are the right things to do, and we just need to ensure their experiences reinforce those beliefs.

Have fun, believe you can do it, and believe your organization can achieve sustainable improvement and results.

Are you brave enough to BELIEVE and create the right reinforcing experiences?

Appendices

Shingo Underlying Truths

Shingo Model Dimension	Principle	SHINGO Definition Fundamental Truth	Morgan Underlying Belief
Enterprise Alignment	Create Value for the Customer	Trust is sacred.	Customers must trust us.
	Create Constancy of Purpose	Our success depends upon a commitment to a shared understanding of why we exist.	The WHY we exist as a team/orgainization gives us commitment to work to this common goal.
	Think Systemically	As we see how and why everything is connected to, or part of, something else, it helps us to better understand, predict and control outcomes.	Seeing the inter-connectedness of work enables better outcomes.
Continuous Improvement	Seek Perfection	People have an innate desire and ability to improve that is only limited by their expectations.	People have an innate desire and ability to improve that is only limited by their expectations.
	Improve Flow and Pull	Eliminating obstacles maximizes value creation.	Eliminating waste maximizes value creation.
	Assure Quality at Source	Quality is perfected through ownership and connectedness.	Quality is striving to get it right.
	Focus on Process	Great processes set people up to succeed.	Great processes set people up to succeed.
	Embrace scientific thinking	The best decisions are based on a clear understanding of reality.	The best decisions are based on a clear understanding of reality.
Cultural Enablers	Lead with Humility	All growth requires vulnerability.	All growth requires vulnerability.
	Respect every individual	Everyone has more capability they can utilize Approval from others	Everyone has more capability they can utilize.

189

Shingo Model Dimension	Principle	SHINGO Definition Behavioural Benchmark
Enterprise Alignment	Create Value for the Customer	**Relate:** We build relationships with our customers to meet and anticipate their needs and align our objectives to them. **Value:** We investigate what our customers really value and we communicate that through the whole organization. **Measure:** We measure to know where we are in relation to our objectives.
	Create Constancy of Purpose	**Align:** Our common sense of purpose drives all of our decisions. **Clarify:** Our contribution to society is so clear to everyone that it unifies our organization. **Communicate:** We know our purpose for existing and how it unifies us, and this is evident in our daily actions and communications
	Think Systemically	**Optimize:** We consider how improvements in our area need to align with improvements in the whole organization. **Impact:** We know how our work impacts the work of others.
Continuous Improvement	Seek Perfection	**Mindset:** We challenge our paradigms and expectations. **Structure:** We approach improvement in a structured way
	Improve Flow and Pull	**Uninterrupted:** We design our work toward continuous creation of value. **Demand:** We produce in response to actual customer demand. **Eliminate:** We systematically look for ways to identify and remove waste from our processes
	Assure Quality at Source	**Mistake-proof:** Our processes are designed to prevent, reveal, and immediately resolve any problem. **Ownership:** Employees feel personally connected to the quality of their work processes and outcomes. **Connect:** We ensure that people are able to see how their work impacts the work of others.
	Focus on Process	**Understand:** We go to where the work happens to develop a thorough understanding of the process. **Design:** We design our processes to minimize waste. **Attribution:** We first look at the process when solving a problem instead of blaming people.
	Embrace scientific thinking	**Reflect:** We understand that decisions and changes are based on careful examination of problems, challenges, and opportunities. **Analyze:** We experiment, innovate, and make decisions with an appropriate analysis of good data and facts. **Collaborate:** We actively seek insight and ideas, especially from those closest to the work.

Believe

Shingo Model Dimension	Principle	SHINGO Definition Behavioural Benchmark
Cultural Enablers	Lead with Humility	**Servant Leadership:** Leaders consider the needs of others first.
	Respect every individual	**Support:** We invest in everyone's development and encourage them to realize their potential.
		Recognize: We honor the contributions of every employee.
		Community: Our organization cares for the community by providing a physically and emotionally safe workplace for employees and by being a good steward to the environment.

Unerlying Beliefs 4+2

Dimen-sions	Aspect to observe	Ideal Behaviours	Description	Underlying Belief
Your Role	As a Coach	I spent time developing my team members. I celebrate and recognize my team with enthusiasm. I use reward systems to recognize ideal behaviours in an unbiased way.	As leader, my main role is to coach my team to be better every day.I adjust my WILO to give them quality time and helps them realize their growth path in short and long-term	Success is letting others develop their ideas and solutions
	As a Facilitator	I seek resources to support my team. I act as a servant leader	As leader, I manage department resources to enable initiatives my team are developing.I challenge current systems to facilitate daily work	Removing road blocks helps teams be successful
Your Actions	Are Consistent	I am predictable and my team trust in consistency on the way I act.	My team, my peers, my leaders see me as someone who keeps his word and is consequent with any act over time.	Consistent habitual behaviour creates culture
	Are Effective	I pursuit do things simpler for my team	As leader, I work to keep systems as simpler and effective as it can. Pursuit sustainable outcomes through ideal behaviours guide my actions.	Making it easier to do the right thing than the wrong thing
Your Words	Are Thoughtful	I care what I say, what the other's listen and confirm understanding	As leader, I put attention on the way I connect and communicate with people. I listen twice that I speak. My words are coming thinking in what the other hear, not what I believe I said.	Big ears and small mouth, my people can teach me
	Are Empowering	I communicate in a confident way; my team can feel my commitment to them	As leader, I use my word to empower and support my team in the decisions they make.	Fostering a safe to fail, learn from failing environment

192

Believe

Dimensions	Aspect to observe	Ideal Behaviours	Description	Underlying Belief
Your Knowledge	Are Curious	I embrace and promote scientific thinking in myself and my team I want to learn from my teams	As leader, I challenge the way I think. I guide my team to follow scientific methods to solve problems and bring new and innovating solutions. And to understand and learn from our people	My people know the answers
	Is Growing	I want to learn every day, for everybody, with open mind and no biases.	As leader, I use Gemba's, go & see and any interaction with my team to learn from them. I give space to my team to strengthen their skills and unlock new ones.	Fostering and creating a learning environment
Your Decisions	Are fact based	I make decision based on evidence, avoiding act with bias	As leader, I use information and data to make decisions, if I don't know I go to confirm my hypothesis. With my team, I give them free space to put facts over the table and help them to realize when we are acting by biases.	Thereare always two sides to a story to understand reality
	Are inclusive	I listen and invite others to share their opinions before making any decision	As leader, I listen and invite others to share their opinions before making any decision. With my team, I embrace and create a safety and respectful environment to share their thoughts and believes.	Everyone has a voice and are deserving to be heard

Dimensions	Aspect to observe	Ideal Behaviours	Description	Underlying Belief
Your Team	Is aligned	I use purpose to inspire my team and be all aligned under same principles	As leader, I use purpose to inspire my team and be all aligned under same principles. My team is aligned by conviction, not by obligation.	Connection and constancy of purpose is for everyone, and it guides our decisions
	Is committed	I left space to my team member to be themselves, building an environment where they can commit between them and with the organization	As leader, I left space to my team member to be themselves, building an environment where they can commit between them and with the organization. My team is committed with the organization and with their teams. The commitment is both personal and as a group.	My people are business owners in their own right

Underlying Beliefs of Coaching Framework

	Habit 1 – Visual Management (VM)	Habit 2 – Huddles	Habit 3 – Continuous Improvement (CI)	Habit 4 – Standard Work (SW)	Habit +1 Lean Leader Walks (Gemba)	Habit +2 Strategy Deployment (SD)
High-Level Definition	Habit of continually updating performance data	Short, sharp performance dialogue addressing gaps and trends	Enabling teams to fix problems at root cause within the realm of control.	Lock in new improvements and confirm improvements materialized and moving metrics on VMB.	Leaders were going to see where the work was done and coach teams to solve the problem where the work was done.	Strategy is broken down by level so that each level of the organization can align the daily work to deliver on strategic measures.
Purpose/ Aim/Intent	Enabling what conversations does the team want to have in the huddle?	Identify opportunities for continuous improvement and Gemba	Use common structured problem solving to fix problems at root cause and test solutions.	Verify improvements moving metrics. Lock in solutions into BAU	Need to see reality. Learn from where the work is done.	Provide clarity of improvement engine to deliver on business strategy, vision, and purpose.
Underlying Beliefs	We understand what value in the eyes of our customers is, so they trust us. It is respectful to have up-to-date data to enable the team to make the best decisions. We use the 1-3-10 rule to drive data transparency and inform the Go and See.	Everyone on the team should know how well things are going, i.e., winning or losing. The team is better at identifying improvements than one individual through Gemba.	Improvement is part of who we are. It is done by everyone every day and everywhere in the organization. Working on the right improvements is pivotal to delivering our strategy. We constantly seek perfection and challenge our aspirational targets. We work collaboratively with all stakeholders to deliver value.	Working as intended and following our processes, standards, procedures, and systems of work will enable us to deliver our strategy and value to the customer.	We need to see reality and learn from where the work is done and from those performing the work. We share and communicate the lessons obtained from the Gemba to create value for our people and the customer.	We are disciplined in ensuring we maintain our SD and DM routines because long-term SD and DM built on our purpose, behaviors, and systems are pivotal to our success. We serve our customers through our actions.

195

	Habit 1 – Visual Management (VM)	Habit 2 - Huddles	Habit 3- Continuous Improvement (CI)	Habit 4 – Standard Work (SW)	Habit +1 Lean Leader Walks (Gemba)	Habit +2 Strategy Deployment (SD)
Ideal Behaviors	Regularly update data and metrics, including customer value proposition and VoC. All team members regularly update data and metrics, including customer value proposition and VOC. Leaders ensure the right KPIs are in place to drive transparency and improvement dialogue. All team members ensure appropriate actions are in place and up to date to close the gaps.	The team has short, focused performance reviews, ideally a 15-minute standing. Discussing Gaps, i.e., red and green trends. Teams have short, focused performance discussions, ideally 15 minutes, standing. Discussing the gaps, i.e., reds and green trends. Teams collaborate as a diverse group to make informed decisions.	Teams identify improvement everywhere, every day. Teams collaborate across the organization to ensure improvement is not done in silos. Teams focus on the green as much as the red, seeking to understand the gaps in aspiration. Teams develop, maintain, and improve systems of work to ensure continuous improvement.	Teams follow standard work processes and procedures. Teams conduct verification activities to measure impact and identify improvement opportunities.	We go to the Gemba, with "Big Eyes, Big Ears and Small Mouth." We go to the Gemba to understand the problem and understand or obtain the solution from those who do the work. We recognized ideal behaviors at the Gemba and addressed non-ideal behaviors.	Leaders link vision, mission, purpose, behaviors, systems, and strategy deployment to business outcomes. Leaders and team members embrace VOC thinking. Leaders ensure that conversations on both horizontal and vertical value streams are taking place.
KPIs & KBIs						

	Habit 1 – Visual Management (VM)	Habit 2 - Huddles	Habit 3- Continuous Improvement (CI)	Habit 4 – Standard Work (SW)	Habit +1 Lean Leader Walks (Gemba)	Habit +2 Strategy Deployment (SD)
Tools and Systems	Performance Boards.	Huddle Purpose/Focus. Agenda. 5P's of meetings.	A3 problem solving. Concern strips. Improvement Boards. Ideas Hub.	Standard Work Procedures	Gemba System Map	Strategy Deployment (Hoshin)
Linkage to other habits	What conversations must the team have in their huddles? Identifies the opportunities for the team to start the Go and See. Provides the link to continuous improvement. Drive quality performance conversations at huddles.	Identify areas to solve problems and go to Gemba. Drives conversation from the VMB from identified opportunities for continuous improvement and going to the Gemba.	Conducting improvement from identified gaps on the VMB and improved results linked to strategy and aligned to purpose. Building the skills of our people creates a continuous improvement mindset. Measure and define improvement based on systems of work, procedures, processes, and standards.	Verify results documenting process/ procedure improvements. Standard work becomes the basis for future improvement. Systems underpin our strategy and the work we do.	Process to inform problem-solving and continuous improvement. Broaden understanding of potential gaps in actual work performed and alignment to work as intended.	Providing the 'why' behind the metrics on the VMB. Ensuring we are working on the right improvement at the right time. We should show the customer that we care about their value. Align all mindsets on performance and confirm KPIs and KBI golden threat.

197

References

Arbinger Institute (2019), The Outward Mindset, Berret-Koehler Publishing.

Berinato, S. (2020). *The restorative power of ritual*. Harvard Business Review. Retrieved May 13, 2024, from https://hbr.org/2020/04/the-restorative-power-of-ritual

Blazej M. Baczkowski, Jan Haaker, Lars Schwabe (2023), Inferring danger with minimal aversive experience, Trends in Cognitive Sciences, Volume 27, Issue 5, Pages 456-467.

Branson, Richard (2011), Losing My Virginity: How I Survived, Had Fun, and Made a Fortune Doing Business My Way, Currency Publishing.

Colotla, Ian, Fookes William, Iverson Ted, Schaefer Erik, Sellschop Richard and Wijpkema Joris, (2023), Today's good to great: Next-generation operational excellence, Retrieved April 3, 2024, www.mckinsey.com.

Duhigg, C. (2012). *The power of habit: Why we do what we do in life and business*. Random House.

Garrett, James, or Brain-by-design (2024), *How to break bad habits in 5 easy*, Retrieved April 3, 2024, www.brainbydesign.com.

Gentry, William A., Weber, Todd J., and Sadri, Golnaz (2007), *Empathy in the Workplace A Tool for Effective Leadership*.

Kaplan, Robert S., (207) What to ask the person in the mirror, Harvard Business Review. Retrieved April 10, 2024, from What to Ask the Person in the Mirror (hbr.org).

Marquet, L. David (2020), Leadership Is Language: The Hidden Power of What You Say and What You Don't Penguin.

Norton, M. I. (2024). The research-backed benefits of daily rituals. Harvard Business Review. Retrieved May 13, 2024, from https://hbr.org/2024/04/the-research-backed-benefits-of-daily-rituals

Perry, Richard, A. (2023), KBI: Learn what Key Behavior Indicators are, their benefits over KPIs, and how they will build the company culture and brand you have been striving for. Richard A Perry Publisher.

Plenert, Gerhard (2021), Driving the Enterprise to Sustainable Excellence: A Shingo Process Overview, Productivity Press.

Plenert, Gerhard (2017), Discover Excellence: An Overview of the Shingo Model and Its Guiding Principles (The Shingo Model Series Book 1), Productivity Press.

Plenert, Joshua (2023), How We Go: Culture-Centric Leadership, High-Functioning Enterprise. Joshua J. Plenert Publisher.

Shingo, Shigeo, Kaizen, and the Art of Creative Thinking, 2007, Enna Products Corporation and PCS Inc., p. 85-86.

Shingo, Shigeo, The Shingo Production Management System, 1992, Productivity Press Inc., translated by Andrew P. Dillon, p. xxii.

www.ingramcontent.com/pod-product-compliance
Lightning Source LLC
Chambersburg PA
CBHW042314210326
41599CB00038B/7127